Real Talk for Teens

Real Talk for Teens

JUMP-START GUIDE TO GENDER TRANSITIONING AND BEYOND

Seth Jamison Rainess, M.S.

Published by:

Harbor View Press

(A division of For LAN's Sake, Inc.)

ISBN: 978-0-578-40936-8

www.sethrainess.com

"It is never too late to be what you might have been."

George Eliot

(born as Mary Ann Evans)

"One must not conceal any part of what one has recognized to be true."

Albert Einstein

This book contains QR codes for you to access video messages from Seth. Download the appropriate QR Reader App for your phone to hear Seth speak.

6 months
4 years
8 years
19 years
13 years
47 years
24 years
49 years
52 years
First year on T
Today

DISCLAIMER

This book was written to help youth deal with issues of transitioning, including becoming aware of their gender identity, transitioning to their preferred gender identity, and living a happy, joyous life beyond their transition. Gender identity is an inner sense of being female, male, neither, or both. Children often have a clear sense of either being male or female by the time they're three years old. Most the time their identity conforms to their biological sex; whether this is the case or the child is transgender, society instills rules in them about how one should conform to their birth sex.

I am a speaker and educator who transitioned later in life because opportunities for gender reassignment were limited in the 1960s, and I know from firsthand experience the importance of transitioning early in life. The suggestions I offer in this book culminate from many years of personal experience and self-reflection, traveling extensively talking and listening to many trans youth, facilitating conference workshops and groups, and teaching many (adults and children) how to achieve success and happiness.

Today, this is what the scenario looks like for youth in 2015. But it is a constantly changing medical, scientific, and political landscape, which means that you need to stay on top of the literature throughout your journey. Hopefully, this book is a good jumpstart for your journey. Always keep informed and aware of the latest medical advances whether hormones or surgery, if that is your intent. Be your own advocate. Treat your body like a shrine, not a trash can. Most importantly, it is your life. You only get one! Be happy!

As of 2018, the TITLE IX potential changes have not happened. It is advised to follow the current situation to become familiar with the current status.

To any adults who happen to read this book—Remember:

IT ONLY TAKES ONE TO HELP ONE.

DEDICATION

There are just too many people who, in one way or another, had a part in this book. Why? Because they have either had, or currently have, a part in my life. They have been integral in helping me to live/survive the earlier part of my life on the other side. They have added to my life:

- Joy and sorrow;
- An education at the school of hard knocks;
- Love and admiration;
- Strength to rise after a fall—time and time again;
- Confidence to resolve conflicts and to know when to walk away.

Their undying support enables me today to pay it forward to those who can start their transition early so they may live a fulfilled life and not go through what I did to get here.

ACKNOWLEDGEMENTS

Trystan Cotten and Loren Bornstein - thanks for taking the relentless time and effort into making this book what it is. Without your expertise and artistic care, it would not be the same. My hat goes off to you both.

Thanks Aiza Blinder for accentuating the graphics.

Nick Brady – my buddy, who always stayed on top of me to make sure I kept going until this was done. Thanks for always being there with a positive word encouraging me for the better.

Laury Yates – for all the sleepless nights and phone call editing and helping me stay on point over these two long years... (and my whole life).

Laura Wolf and Joan Carbonaro – 3 simple words – I love you.

Jamison Green and Aidan Key for your support and feedback.

Mark Hassman – thanks for calling me weekly to make sure that I stayed the course.

David Davidson – who has whipped me into shape over the past nine years and still continues to push me to be my best.

Theresa - thanks for your support and being another mother to me.

FOREWORD

Some people embrace change; others fear it. It's very possible that there is nothing more exciting—or more frightening—than changing yourself, inside and outside.

If you're a teen who's contemplating, or in the process of, a gender transition, this book has some valuable information for you. Seth Rainess has thought a lot about your circumstances, and he's packed this brief guide with perspective and information that you can really use to help you reach all kinds of goals, transition-related or lifetime-related goals. Either way, you'll find something in here that will benefit you for years to come.

If you're a parent of a teen who's contemplating, or in the process of, a gender transition, you need to know that your child is not the first young person to grapple with their gender identity. Reading this book can help you understand what your child has to think about, and why. It can be very difficult—or frightening—for parents to let go of their expectations for a child and to acknowledge that they never really knew what was possible for that individual.

The unexpected and the unknown can seem daunting, but this book demonstrates that transgender kids can survive, can be wise, and can accomplish something that contributes to society. Transgender kids can be good people. They only need what every other kid needs to succeed: to be seen and to be loved for whom they ARE, to be supported until they have the skills and the resources to be on their own, and to be taught the values that encourage kindness, respect for themselves and others, and that nourish a desire to contribute to society. These are the building blocks that enable people to live with integrity.

Integrity can help protect an individual from self-harm, and it's crucial for building healthy relationships, and for being able to recognize when one is in with the "wrong crowd." Honesty, authenticity, trustworthiness, and capacity for commitment, all are made possible by integrity. And trans people's capacity for integrity is just as great as anyone else's, so don't let your worries about transition cause you to limit your child's options. Your emotional support and openness with your child—and your willingness to allow your teen to be open with you—contributes to their resiliency and integrity.

Rainess offers transgender teens tools for success and guidance about the potential joys and pitfalls ahead when one is trans. The options available for trans teens are variable and subjective, depending on where one resides, how much support one has, how available information and contact with other trans people is. One small book cannot possibly cover everything. There is a HUGE amount of information out there now, on the Web, in the media, in libraries, in support groups around the country, which may meet online or in person. Still, Rainess navigates for the curious and the watchful, ensuring that readers have pointers to help them find their way. What a generous gift! Here is to everyone's safe and rewarding journey.

Jamison Green, PhD
Oakland, California

Table of Contents

ABOUT ME

First things first.

Good news. You don't have to wait forever to transition like me. I didn't have access to the resources and information that you have today. If I had, I would have transitioned as soon as possible and all the mental energy I spent thinking and pining away about being a man could have gone into pursuing other goals. The good news is the world has changed since I was your age. You don't have to wait to transition! You can do it right now, while you're still young, and enjoy a long life in the body that reflects your true self.

You are fortunate to grow up in the world today where LGBTQI[1] people are more visible and taken more seriously. This has led to social and legal changes that now work *for* instead of *against* us.

This means you're in a better place, not only because of those changes, but also because "transgender" is becoming better understood today, and you can more easily get the medical help you need to become you. I know we still have a ways to go to fully change laws and access healthcare, but we've made an incredible leap forward since my childhood.

I'm going to be upfront though: Transitioning is not simple. It has multiple layers. As a teen, because of your age and limited life experience, transition is more difficult than it might be for an adult. However this doesn't mean that it can't be done. You have to be patient and use all resources that are available to

1 Lesbian, Gay, Bisexual, Transgender, Questioning/Queer, Intersex.

you. Some parts of your journey are in your control and other parts are not. I'm going to talk about what *is* in your control—*you*—and how you can start creating the kind of life you want.

Being trans is both unique and universal. If that sounds contradictory, let me explain. Trans people face some of the same struggles in life as cis-gender[2] folks. Most people want to live purposeful lives. We want to love and be loved. Some of us want families and most of us want a community to be a part of and to contribute something to the world. We want to be remembered for something—to leave a legacy—long after we're gone from the planet. Our trans-ness colors the choices we make and the paths we take to realize our purpose in life. For example, trans people have families just like cis-gender people. Some of the paths we take to creating family are like those of cis-gender people, while other paths are different because of our trans-ness.

Transitioning isn't an easy road, but neither is anything else in life. You may encounter a few stumbling blocks in your transition—perhaps you already have—and you may not immediately get everything you want. Some of the best things in life take time to acquire and have to be earned. You'll find that you appreciate them more.

I'm going to talk about some ways that you can get through your transition, including the tough times, by offering you a tool kit built from my own life experiences. I want you to begin living with joy and purpose now, wherever you are in your transition. Some of the information I offer you here may also be useful for dealing with life issues that come up after you've transitioned.

In my line of work, I've seen plenty of suggestions for transgender youth—some of it good, especially the stuff on hormone dosages, surgical techniques and being recognized as the gender you know yourself to be. The problem is most of this information speaks to your parents instead of *you*—the one who is actually going through transition.

Of course, there's value in discussing gender reassignment with adults, because it is often their decision about when your transition will start, and they need to be informed as much as possible. But here's the thing to keep in mind: Your gender isn't about them. *It's about you.* This means you need information and guidance to help get you through the process.

So, here it is. A lifetime of lessons condensed into a book written just for *you* and your unique journey through life as a trans person.

But first, you should know who I am and why I am here to help to you.

Nice to meet you.

I'm Seth, a motivational speaker and life coach. I encourage and teach people how

2 Someone who is not transgender.

to reach their goals. I help all kinds of people, but since I happen to be transgender, I have a special place in my heart for trans people, especially trans teens. I help trans youth reach their transition goals by staying focused and grounded, and by learning to see obstacles as opportunities and problems as possibilities. I also talk to parents about helping their kids' transition early in life because I know all too well that transitioning sooner can often help you focus on reaching other milestones.

Despite transitioning later in the game, I've had a wonderful life. I was lucky to have a career I loved and run my own successful business—be my own boss. I'm an independent man. I own my home and some nice toys like my two motorcycles. I'm also an accomplished musician and have travelled around the world. I've had the opportunity to meet some incredible people from many different cultures. The best part of traveling though is that I get talk to a lot of trans teens like you.

When I was a kid, I had a vague, nagging feeling that something wasn't right between my body and how I felt inside. For years, I felt like I was on the outside of a room looking at everyone else who seemed to be enjoying life so much more than me. I didn't feel like I fit in anywhere, including in my own skin. What was worse was not having words, like *transgender* and *transition* that you have today, to articulate what I felt and needed.

When I turned nine, my parents took me to see one of the most famous doctors in trans history, Dr. John Money, for what I thought was a diagnosis of homosexuality. Back then, homosexuality was considered as a mental illness. Dr. Money was an important researcher who pioneered the study of gender identity[3] in the 1960s and helped establish a transition clinic at Johns Hopkins University to perform sex change operations on adults.

I'll never forget the two pictures he held up in front of me. One was a vagina and the other was a penis. He asked me three simple, yet powerful questions:

1. "Do you know what these are?"
2. "Which one do you have?"
3. "Which one do you want?"

I don't remember exactly what I said, but I do remember I lied. While I wanted a penis and wondered where mine was, I was also old enough to know that, if I had been truthful with Dr. Money about my feelings, my parents probably would have punished me, or worse, I could have been sent to a mental institution because homosexuality (and people who appeared to dress differently

3 Gender identity is an inner sense of being female, male, neither, or both. By the age of 3, children often have a clear sense of either being male or female. Most the time their identity conforms to their biological sex; whether this is the case or the child is transgender, society instills in them rules about one should conform to their birth sex.

than traditional standards) was seen as a mental disease. But that didn't stop my young mind from wondering: *Where was my penis?*

While I couldn't change my body, I didn't let it get me down. Instead, I hoped to find a solution for my dysphoria[4] someday and went on with life, throwing myself into numerous hobbies and projects. I enjoyed spending time with my family and friends and looked forward to a having a family of my own one day. I worked hard in school so I could make a successful career for myself.

Even though the word *"transgender"* wasn't used back then, I moved in a more masculine direction as I grew older. But that nagging feeling of being on the outside looking in continued to linger into adulthood until I found a gay community and came out as a lesbian thinking that would quell my underlying feelings. I didn't know gender reassignment was possible. Everyone kept telling me I was a woman, a masculine woman, but a *woman* nonetheless.

I spent a lot of those years wishing I was someone else. Until people have concrete life tools and solid ideas of how to move forward with life, we do the best with the bodies and surroundings we have. I lived that lesbian identity for 30 years but it never quite fit with my internal male self. Eventually, I became exhausted trying to be someone I wasn't. My energy was sapped from thinking about the things most of the world took for granted: Being in the body that matched my mind. My wife (at the time) used to ask me, "WHEN IS ENOUGH, ENOUGH?" I thought it was about working and working to make money. It wasn't until after we separated, that I came to realize it was about not being happy inside.

Finally, after finding a name for my condition, transgender, and a health system to get the body I should have had, I didn't waste any more time. I took the right steps and started hormone replacement therapy (HRT) and found surgeons to give me the male body I'd always wanted. I've never looked back or felt more alive since!

Transitioning later in the game.

One advantage of transitioning later in life was that I'd had more life experience than you to meld my character and give me wisdom and strength. Another advantage was that I was grown and didn't need anyone's permission to become a man. So I was able to make decisions about my transition that didn't require conversations with my parents or their consent. I'll talk later about how you can communicate with your parents and other adults to meet your transition goals.

Although I've lived a wonderful life, I would have transitioned earlier—if I'd known it was possible. There were no guidebooks back then, just a handful of doctors like Dr. Money quietly working with a few trans patients on the down-low. Trans wasn't high profile in the media like today. Things were hush-hush. That's why I

4 Dysphoria means "a state of feeling unhappy, or experiencing emotional or mental discomfort." Gender dysphoria occurs when there is a 'disconnect' on some level with all or some gendered aspects of a transgender person's body.

wrote this book for you, so that you can live your entire life as the person you truly are.

You don't have to stumble around in the dark searching for the right diagnosis and support like my generation. Nor do you have to hurry either. You can transition at whatever pace is comfortable for you. The point I'm making is that you have a lot more resources at your disposal than I did.

Having a vocabulary (*"trans," "transgender,"* etc.) for what you're feeling helps you find other people, including medical and legal services, who can support you. Today, there are doctors, surgeons, psychiatrists, social advocates and researchers who will back up your feelings with scientific information that wasn't available when I was a kid.

What does this all mean for you? You're going to be able to transition and be yourself earlier in life!

Perhaps you want to transition now, but it feels like transitioning is a long ways off. You may be under 18 years old and/or need money and feel you'll have to wait forever to get the chance to transition, but imagine waiting decades like me. I remember something my grandmother used to say: *"All good things come in time."* This was her way of helping me stay focused and patient about something, while also reassuring me that change can, and does occur, even when I couldn't see it.

I'm not going to sugarcoat things though. Gender reassignment isn't simple and neither is life. I wish I could promise you that everything will go exactly as you want, but life rarely moves in a simple straight line. Transitioning is no different. It's a *process* that takes time. Sometimes you'll encounter setbacks that are beyond your control, and you'll need tools to help you deal with those moments to help keep your eyes on the bigger picture.

Being unable to change my body or circumstance as a young man in a female body pushed me to think deeply about what I could and could not control. I kept coming back to the same question: *How could I deal with whatever comes my way and have a happy life despite my predicament?* Regardless of my body, I knew I wanted more in life. I wanted to be a man I could be proud of—a successful man, a strong man, a morally upstanding man and someone who others could depend upon.

Some of the tool kit I'm sharing with you comes from those years of my life when I couldn't transition and had to make the best of my situation. I had to grow tough alligator skin, so to speak, and learned a few tricks of how to stay strong.

CHAPTER 1

Developing Your Mental Toolkit for Life

While you are trying to figure out who you are, what you stand for, and who you want to be, there are many attributes of your personality that you need to develop and incorporate into your daily behavior. Like a carpenter who uses tools to build things, the toolkit I'm offering in this book can help you build important character virtues while you transition and find happiness in life. Not losing sight of who you are as you transition is very important. You don't want transitioning to become the sole focus of your life. While transitioning is a priority, you have to continue to develop other traits and virtues that will help you in all other areas of life.

Alligator Skin.

First, you'll learn to grow some *"alligator skin,"* something my mother was fond of saying. What she meant was that I needed to develop some mental armor to surround myself—a protective plate that's tough but also flexible—to live a successful, fulfilling life. You don't want to cut yourself off from other people, because connection with others is part of what makes you human. At the same time, you can't let prejudiced people get to you. Develop the inner strength you need to repel the haters, but be open enough to others so you can develop fully as a human being. When you're in the middle of something difficult—an argument with your parents, some kid harassing you, or disappointment getting transition-related healthcare—it helps to be able to take what

you need out of it and leave the rest. Because, let's face it: Life isn't easy. It never stops moving forward, and curveballs are always coming at you. You just learn to dodge them better.

Growing alligator skin will help you build character and strength and prevent haters from getting under your skin. Along with confidence comes self-esteem, which allows you to hold your head up high and deal with the choices you make in any circumstance. You will be able to reinforce these traits by taking responsibility for the things that you say and do.

Integrity and honesty.

Taking responsibility will also help you build your integrity and honesty. By learning to respond thoughtfully rather than react impulsively to situations, you'll be able to make wiser decisions about your transition and other situations that come up in life. Amazingly enough, integrity and honesty come into play when you are questioning your gender identity. Understand that people can change their behavior and attitudes to please other people, but it could mean that they're not being true to themselves. To have integrity you must be honest with yourself and others. In other words, you talk the talk and walk the walk. Most importantly, you do the right thing even if it is not the easiest or most popular path. When you are honest with people, it means that you also are sincere. Along with having a sense of honor, you are not only honest on the outside but on the inside as well. Don't lie to anyone, and more importantly, don't lie to yourself. Integrity is the most important trait in your mental toolkit and life. It is the major reason and driving force that enables you to be the real you.

Failure and success.

If there is anything in life that you should take seriously, it is how you respond to failure. Quitting has never been in my vocabulary. From the time I was little, I constantly heard from my mother: "If at first you don't succeed, try, try again." That was her antidote to everything, especially, when it came to school and certain subjects that I hated. She would say, "If you quit now, what are you going to do when things really get hard in life?" She meant that if I quit I'd never develop the skills necessary to succeed. I hated hearing her say that back then, but I am thankful for it today because it helped strengthen my work ethic and problem solving skills. Looking back, it always amazes me how often my mother was right.

At times, you'll experience failure too. Everyone does at some point in their lives.

But failure shouldn't paralyze you. Instead, it should *mobilize* you. Failure is an opportunity to learn from your mistakes so you can make better decisions in the future. Things rarely go as smoothly as we plan and you'll encounter obstacles in your life. But remember, even though you occasionally fall, every time you get up you have made progress toward your goal. Failure can help you grow alligator skin. Some situations have straightforward solutions. Other situations like transitioning may not. You may have to search and try several options until you find the right one that works for you.

By learning how to handle failure, you will also build your **self-confidence.** Strong people are made by hard work and constant effort regardless of their failures. The media makes you think that success depends solely on inherent talent. The truth is, most successes are built on a string of failed attempts followed by the determination to stay the course. Success in any area depends on your willingness to move forward.

There's no such thing as a mistake.

If situations don't go as you planned or hoped, you can still learn something from them. All failures contain valuable nuggets of knowledge to make you wise. So look for the lessons in them by asking yourself:

- "What was my role?"
- "What did I miss or didn't anticipate?"
- "How can I do this differently the next time?"

Exploring these questions gives you something to think about and an opportunity to rethink your strategy.

Chances are you will not make perfect decisions.

Why? Because there's no such thing as perfect and trying to be perfect puts unnecessary pressure on you. Just do your best.

Never accept mediocrity. Experiencing repeated failure may make you want to settle or give up. But don't give in or sell yourself short, because mediocrity will only hold you back from discovering your higher potential and purpose. Many people will try to steer you to become *their* version of perfect. A prime example is gender. How many times has someone tried to mold you into *their* ideal of what a girl or boy should be? How did it feel? It was frustrating for me. You know it's wrong, so don't do that to yourself!

So if failure is a friend?

Why does it feel so bad? It's likely because you haven't been taught that failure is a good way to succeed.

Failure is merely an event. It doesn't *describe* who you are. Nor is it you! The problem comes when you quit. Quitting means you have given up and allowed yourself to become a victim rather than a survivor and it becomes easier to blame anything that goes wrong on someone else rather than take responsibility for your part.

Attitude—negative and positive.

Your attitude will not take care of itself without some attention. You need to be conscious of it every day. When you encounter negativity in the world, stay positive and resist the impulse to be pulled down by it. Say something positive in every conversation. Remove negative words ("can't," won't," "impossible") from your vocabulary. It may not be easy at first, but it can definitely be achieved. Even if you only replace a few negative words with positive ones, you will start to feel better about yourself. Here is how to start:

Replace:	With:
• I CAN'T	• I CAN—I WILL
• IF ONLY	• I KNOW—ABSOLUTELY
• I DON'T THINK	• I AM SURE
• MAYBE	• I AM CONFIDENT

Most importantly: Be positive.[5]

- Choose to be optimistic: Work to remain positive. Learn to accept things as they are. That does not mean you will give up. Just move forward.
- Choose to be enthusiastic: Look for excitement in every day. The more upbeat you are, others around you will be the same.

---

5 Paraphrased from: *What do You Stand For? For Teens*, Barbara A. Lewis.

- Choose to be cheerful: Don't say gloomy things. Think before you speak. When you are positive you will attract positive people—those likely to support you.
- Choose to have a sense of humor: If something is silly don't miss the opportunity to laugh. More importantly, be able to laugh at yourself.
- Choose to be humble: Be interested in others beside yourself.
- Choose to be grateful: Think about the things for which you can be grateful. It makes you feel good about your life and puts a smile on your face.
- Choose to have hope: Life without hope has no meaning. Make sure you set goals and plan. Hope goes along with being optimistic and positive.
- Choose to be caring: Always remember how you feel when others are thoughtful about you. Step outside of yourself and give back whether it is by a small action or saying some kind words. You might be amazed at how good these things will make you feel.

Accountability/responsibility—choices/decisions.

You are responsible for your life, and the decisions you make. Each choice has a consequence. Even with the best of planning, not every decision may be right. You will only realize the result after your action. If it was wrong just admit it.

These are examples that you can think about. You can list the good and bad points of each decision. By doing this, you will be prepared to make better decisions based on the information at hand.

- Going to college versus not going to college
- Getting exercise versus being a couch potato
- Doing homework versus blowing off homework
- Standing up for a person who is being bullied versus ignoring it

If you are under 18 and your parents are making the decisions about your transition, it is important for you to contribute to the process. When it comes to school and your friends, you have more control than you think over the decisions you make. If you relinquish control and allow your friends to make decisions for you, you cannot blame them when the outcome is unfavorable. Regardless of the outcome, you are still accountable for your decisions and actions. Don't blame others or lie or make excuses for your behavior.

Responsibility takes many forms:

- Responsibility to your family
- Responsibility to obey the laws
- Responsibility to people, animals and the planet
- Responsibility to your beliefs
- Responsibility to your community
- Responsibility to yourself

All these responsibilities come down to a few basic things. They indicate that you are dependable and that if you say that you are going to do something, you can be counted on by others to do it. This is the case, especially if you are part of a team effort. It means that you show up for practice even if you don't feel like it. You may have certain chores assigned to you at home. Don't whine about them. Just do them. Take time to care for animals, especially if they are family pets. Don't ignore animal abuse or any abuse for that matter. You'll be doing research about your transition. Write down what's important to you. Educate yourself so that you will know all your options and make informed choices. It's part of your responsibility to yourself.

Be Organized.

How do you become organized? Try keeping "to-do" lists. Keep a calendar record of your appointments, tests, practices, and show up on time, and five minutes before when possible. When you arrive at appointments on time, people will respect you and consider you to be a responsible person.

Define your goals. Put them in writing. It'll give you a path to follow and you'll have something concrete to refer to and remind yourself to be accountable and responsible. Remember that things are always changing and you'll need to make adjustments as you go along.

This is the case with anything in life whether you're trying to:

- Reach your full potential
- Transition and feel aligned
- Be a successful business owner
- Save money and help others, or
- Change a bad habit

Planning goals keeps you focused and moving forward, even when it may seem things are not moving at all. You'll be able to look back to see what you've actually accomplished.

During the course of the day and week you'll have to prioritize things by their importance in your life. Some things will happen out of nowhere like getting a flat tire or a friend in crisis, but others, like studying for an exam, or starting your transition, require planning and prioritizing so you can see what *needs to be done immediately* and what can wait. Planning ahead is a key tool to achieving your goals and being successful in any endeavor. When it comes to developing yourself, it moves at a gradual and ever-changing pace.

Responding versus Reacting.

If you think about it, life is just a never-ending series of situations. Situations automatically prompt us to counter first with our emotions (happy, angry, sad, neutral) and then with our actions. What do all these situations have in common? *It's up to you to choose how you handle them.* The route you choose boils down to two options: You can ***respond*** or ***react.***

What's the difference?

Responding to a situation means you take a moment to think through how you'll act without emotions. You check in with your principles to help guide your action. Don't rely on what others think you should do, either. Try to remain calm and be fair. You must learn to accept that things will happen sometimes that are beyond your control. But what you *can* control is how you handle and respond to them.

Reacting is different from responding. Reacting is doing the first and easiest thing that comes to mind. It is impulsive–racing into a situation with your emotions rather than your mind controlling you. Your ability to listen, look, and process the details of a situation often slows down or stops working altogether. Being emotional can also lead you to blaming someone or something else for what's happening if things aren't going your way. Reacting usually makes the situation worse.

Reactive responses keep you stuck in bad moods; they push others away and often lead to regret. They also undermine your ability to reach your goals.

Respond instead of react. Think about situations where you've been losing your cool or making snap decisions. Replay the events over again in your head, focus on *your* words and actions, and think about what you could have done or said differently to lead to a different outcome. This is how you learn to take control over situations. Recognize, too, how easily the situation got out of control, so you can be prepared to respond better the next time. You learn and grow by focusing on the things that are in your control—namely, your responses. It may feel impossible at first, but you have to learn to control your emotions, otherwise other people and events will control you. Discipline is an invaluable tool if you want to be successful in life, whether that's meeting your transition goals, pursuing a career path, raising your own family, or inventing something new.

That doesn't mean overlook your feelings.

It's important to express and work through your feelings because if you don't, they'll come back to haunt you later. You'd be surprised how often we're not actually letting ourselves *feel* the full extent of our sadness or frustration. Instead, we replay the same interaction in our minds and imagine how it would go differently. We beat ourselves down or feel too embarrassed to face it head on. We worry that the full force of our feelings (really letting ourselves scream, sob, laugh, smile...etc.) will be overwhelming so we push it away.

Have you ever done any of these things? I certainly have.

One of the *keys* to letting yourself actually feel your feelings is to know that you don't have to do it alone. You don't have to sit in your room alone dealing with your pain, whether it's fear, anger or loss. There are people you can talk to. They can give you valuable feedback for how to deal with situations if and when you have to confront them again. You just have to find them. Also, there are hotlines you can call if your emotions feel too overwhelming. *(See Appendix II)* Talking our feelings out loud can sometimes help us understand them better. I'm amazed how many times I've gone over a situation in my mind's eye with no resolution in sight, and it was only when I voiced it out loud that I could finally see a path forward!

If you're not ready to open up to someone else, you can write about your feelings in a private journal or diary, or make a video series, where you can express your thoughts and feelings more openly. You may feel creative and write a poem, song, or prose. Perhaps drawing or some other artistic format can help you work through your feelings.

Keep a notebook of your feelings because it provides a safe space for you to express yourself. It is also a record of the progress you've made in your transition and life in general. You can look back at any time and see how far you've come. It's a written record of all the challenges you have overcome—evidence of your character becoming *stronger* and *more resilient*.

Resilience–adversity–being unique.

Transgender people have to be very tough—*trans tough*. It takes a lot of guts when you feel like a square peg in a round hole to walk to the beat of your own drum. There are many rewards for being your true self: an inner peace and resilience that will sustain you through the tough times.

Life can feel stifling at your age sometimes, like you're inside a plastic bag trying to fight your way out. You can see out of it but can't get free. I know that can feel extremely frustrating. I've been inside that bag myself.

But there's a flip side to most things in life. Fighting for release brings its rewards: It teaches us to be strong. The more adversity you work through the more strength you build to deal with issues down the road.

Being trans means you're unique. Distinct. And that's good, despite what you may read or hear from others or the media. You don't look like anybody else, nor do you need to act like anybody else. You stand out from other people. Now everybody seems to think that if you stand out from the pack you're... What? Weirdo. Geek. Nerd. Freak. You can become a target for being different. Why? You're already doing something that a lot of your peers are going to take years to achieve: You are thinking for yourself. You have your own mind and that means you're actually ahead of the game and a lot less likely to fall in with a dangerous crowd or be blindly led by other people. It also means that once you've jumped over some hurdles, you feel a freedom many people only dream about.

Navigating peer pressure.

Of course, I know I don't have to tell you about peer pressure. You've already heard a ton about it from your parents, teachers, and the Internet and you have possibly experienced it as well.

However, when it comes to navigating peer pressure, the point isn't to avoid what others tell you is cool at all costs. Rather it's about developing the skill of discerning what works for you and being able to let go of the rest. It's about using your toolkit. As a transgender person, you're already set up with internal drives to do just that.

You have the potential to be a leader. You're able to do things without getting the go-ahead from anyone else. Does that mean that every single person who's different is going to be a trailblazer? The next Laverne Cox or Caitlyn Jenner? Heck no. Frankly, most of us don't want to be in the limelight. We just want to live our lives fully and make contributions to whatever part of the world we're in, and it's admirable to be a piece of the puzzle no matter how large or small. All you need to do is stake a claim to your authentic self and make that clear to others. Believe me, people will listen, though maybe not all of them at first.

If everyone acts and looks the same, not only would our world be filled with robots—and not the cool movie kind—but the world would be a very bland and dreary place. If everybody thought the same and had the same opinion, there would be no innovation or invention. Life wouldn't get better because society would still be thinking the same backwards way it did back in the Stone Age.

We all get handed some tough lots in life, but it's up to you to take lemons and turn them into lemonade. If you keep pushing through adversity, success is on the other side. Success isn't simply measured by material possessions though. It's this internal sense of wholeness that doesn't have a price tag. Use your toolkit and you will succeed in transition and in life.

CHAPTER 2

Coming Out

Ok, so you've uncovered a new, thrilling dimension of yourself. Now what? Should you tell someone? Who do you tell and how do you start that conversation? What if you don't get the supportive response you were hoping for? What if they don't understand? What if they reject you?

Before we can discuss coming out though, we need to go over three important terms. By understanding these, it will help clarify your thoughts and feelings.

- ***Gender Identity*** *is an inner sense of being female, male, neither, or both. By the age of three, children often have a clear sense of either being male or female.*
- ***Gender Expression*** *refers to the ways in which people externally communicate their gender identity to others through behavior, clothing, haircut, voice, and other forms of presentation.*
- ***Sexual Orientation*** *is about romantic and sexual attraction; it is not a choice. It has nothing to do with gender identity or gender expression; orientation is about how one finds others attractive, while gender identity and expression are about how one perceives and manifests the self. Everyone has both a sexual orientation and a gender identity.*

As a teen, the idea of transitioning can be daunting. It is what I call an "adult problem" that you are now facing as a teen with limited life experience.

The need to transition physically adds a unique dimension to coming out for many trans people. Why? Because *unlike coming out about sexuality, being trans often isn't just about wanting people to know: It's also about wanting to change your body, too.*

Once we accept our trans identity, sometimes we feel a rush to tell family and friends. We may feel elated and want others to share in our joy. Remember, you don't have to rush to come out. Telling others about your trans identity will be some of the biggest conversations of your life, depending on who you're talking to and the circumstances. It's important to take some time and reflect on *who* you want to tell and *when* and *where* those conversations should take place. You'll need to gather your strength ahead of time in case the conversation doesn't go as smoothly as you'd like. It takes more than a day to push out the negative messages about trans people. **Take the time you need** to get over the negative hype and work through any bad feelings about being trans you may be holding inside. Coming out is something you want to do feeling comfortable and confident. Gathering your composure beforehand will help you respond effectively rather than emotionally.

Even though being trans *isn't* a choice, we *do* have choices about whom, when, and how we tell others. Each person we consider talking to has a different way of reacting to news. The best way to deal with any situation is to plan ahead. Here are a few helpful things to remember:

- **Be emotionally strong and stable.** You need to have a firm emotional footing before coming out to handle people's reactions. Sometimes you'll get annoying questions about your personal life from people, or hear a remark that sounds ignorant. It's important that you are strong enough emotionally to handle these situations in a cool manner and not let them get to you.

- **Come out to yourself first.** You may feel excited and want to tell everyone, or hesitant and unsure of who to tell. Either way, take a moment to enjoy this new discovery of yourself. Breathe. Relax. You will need to do your own research to confirm that this is what you are feeling. You can refer to *Appendices IV & VII* to get some good reading material. You are certainly not the only one and there are many resources that will help you to understand your feelings.

- **Know that everything will ultimately work out the way it's supposed to.** Remember, you're working toward being your whole, true self and some people may not be ready to come along for the ride just yet. You cannot worry about them; for they may (or may not) come to accept you.

- **Keep in mind, your body language.** Your body says as much about your intentions as the words you speak. It's important that you show confidence when coming out. Look people in the eye when you're talking. Avoid squirming, shrugging, and looking down at the floor. It's okay to be nervous, that's normal, but your body language doesn't have to show it.

Coming out to your world first.

Think about the important people in your world—the people who matter the most to you. Make a list if that helps.

- *My parents (or guardian)...*
- *My siblings...*
- *My friends...*
- *My teachers...*
- *My employer and co-workers...*

Ask yourself: How will they react? Does the idea of coming out to any of these people feel a little scary? If so, that's okay. These are important people in your life—people you love and care about—and it's perfectly reasonable to feel anxious. After all, you don't know how they're going to react. The reality is trans youth can (and are) bullied, harassed, and experience emotional and physical violence at home, school and in the streets when they open up to others about their trans identity, and even when they don't disclose. Some youth are abused and forbidden to talk about their trans identity, even kicked out of their homes or schools, or feel they have to run away. While these things don't happen to everyone, they could happen to you and **your safety and well-being are the first things you must always consider before coming out**.

That doesn't mean that every coming out experience is going to be dangerous and terrifying. **Some will be exciting and empowering**. You'll get better at coming out because each time you'll learn something from people's reactions that will make you wiser for the next occasion.

While coming out is definitely a positive thing, it's also life-altering. The best way to do so is to plan ahead and proceed cautiously instead of blazing forward.

Most trans people will have at least one person in their life that has a hard time wrapping their head around gender nonconformity and reassignment. For example, while most of my experiences of coming out were positive, I was surprised by the reaction from a pair of friends I'd known for a long time whom I considered liberal. I thought they'd be happy for me, but they said that they needed time to process my new identity. Sadly, I never heard from them again. Even though I was still the same person inside—just a little happier and peaceful—their progressive politics apparently only extended so far.

It can hurt to know that even while you're finally embracing and becoming your true self, others who you care about may not be ready or willing to come along with you on your journey right away. People's levels of acceptance and understanding of your gender identity can take time. They may need a while to adjust to the information you're giving them, and this is especially the case if you're asking them to use new pronouns and call you by a new name. Remember, they are also transitioning with you.

Build confidence and ease with coming out by telling people who are most likely to accept you and go with the flow. Think about the *safest* place and people you can come out to and leave the more difficult people who you think will respond with confusion, denial, or anger for later, until after you've had a few successful experiences. So, let's talk about how to prepare.

To gauge a situation, ask yourself some questions:

Do I feel safe?

If you think there's any chance that you'll be harassed, threatened, physically harmed, then stay away from those environments and people. They aren't *safe.* This doesn't mean you can't ever come out to them, but it's not safe to do so right now.

What's my home life like?

Are your parents generally okay with changes? How is conflict and disagreement handled in your family? Do your parents take the time to talk things through with you? How do they take new information? Are they respectful? Do they yell? Do they react physically to off-putting news?

If you get the sense that your parents may become violent, the hard truth is you may want to consider waiting to come out to them until after you've left home, or at least until you know there's somewhere else you can go if things turn badly. Understand that abuse isn't just physical. It's also *emotional* and includes verbal threats, demeaning insults, berating you, putting down your humanity, and making you feel worthless.

The bottom line: Never tell someone you're trans if you feel you will be harmed.

Your safety is important.

Family can be one of the biggest supports in your life and if you feel safe and comfortable coming out to family members, then do so. Sometimes it can be helpful to turn to a sibling first if you have a good relationship with them and know they will be on your side. That doesn't mean the conversations will be easy. In fact, they can be tough at times, but they *will* be worth it. It is wise to have a good understanding of your sibling relationship because if you confide in them, they could use it against you and out you if things turn sour between you.

What are my friends like?

You may be thinking of coming out to your friends first and there's an advantage to telling peers. Unlike adults, peers, like siblings, are in your age group and may be more likely to go with the flow of your transition. Hopefully, you'll find some who'll be happy for you, offer their support and will have your back in difficult situations. Friends are the most likely people to begin immediately using your preferred name and new pronouns.

However, be careful; and come out first to the people who'll most likely accept you. Once you do, be sure to tell them to keep your trans identity to themselves until you give them permission to tell others. A true friend will let you tell others in your own time and doesn't spread rumors or the details of your personal life and identity.

You probably have some friends online, too. There's lots of great support on Facebook, YouTube, Tumblr and Twitter. If you reach out and start to chat or email another trans person, this can be a good outlet for you to express your feelings, frustrations, and triumphs. You can also ask other trans people what their coming out experiences were like and what strategies worked best for them. But be wary of giving out your personal contact information, like your phone number, address, or your real name, when communicating with people on the Internet, because you can't always be sure of the person's real identity.

What's my school environment like?

How do you determine whether or not your school environment is safe to come out in? One way, is to observe your classmates' and teachers' attitudes about other kinds of diversity. Do you go to a school where people accept different cultures, languages, disabilities, and appearances? Does your school have multicultural clubs or a Gay/Straight Alliance? What is the social climate and how do students feel about these groups? It is good to know who these students are and which teachers oversee these groups because they may be allies who will help you.

These are some important things to consider when assessing your safety and the risks of coming out in school. If you go to a school where diversity is uncommon, or isn't welcomed, then it may not be a safe environment for you to come out in.

Gather your support system and resources before deciding to come out in school, if you decide that is the best option. If you do come out in school, be aware you may have to advocate for yourself. If you happen to be working, this is another situation in which you will have to gauge by the atmosphere in your environment. Some employers may be fine with your transition and some may not. You could even be fired. Unfortunately, at this time, there aren't many laws protecting transgender people against discrimination in the workplace.

What's my town like?

The good news is that more cities and states are passing *gender nondiscrimination* ordinances and laws, making it illegal for schools, stores, and employers to discriminate against gender-nonconforming and transgender students, customers, and employees. Do some research on your town and state to see if there are any regulations protecting trans people. This information can be very valuable to you, especially if you need to fight back against harassment or discrimination. (*See Appendix III for TITLE IX law.*) Remember also, to check if your town and state governments agree on trans discrimination, because sometimes they don't, and it's worth the extra effort to find out by looking it up online. If you have difficulty finding it, ask an adult, a librarian for example, to help you.

Are there other resources near you? Home and school can be safe havens, but when they're not, we need somewhere else to turn. Are there adults or mentors in these places who you can trust and will listen to you?

Does your town (or a town nearby) have an LGBTQI Center? Or an LGBTQI Health Center that specifically caters to queer and trans people? Is there a local hospital, church, or social services that hold groups for trans people to meet and talk about their lives and issues? If so, it's worth seeking them out and find out whether you're comfortable there. Even if you're shy stepping into a new space, remember that these are safe spaces made specifically for people like you. Remember too: Everyone there started out as a stranger!

Even when we make our best-laid plans, sometimes things don't go according to the way we want. It's best to be realistic, so that if you fall short, you have a softer place to land.

Your back-up plan might look like one of these:

- *I'd head to my aunt's house for the weekend.*
- *I'd ask the youth center's advisor to talk to my parents.*

- *I'd turn to a list of hotlines or shelters because I might have to be out of my house.*
- *I'd ask my friends to do some of the talking to classmates for me.*

All of these strategies are excellent examples of thinking ahead and being in control of your transition.

"Can we talk?" Planning your coming out conversation.

Now, that you've done some pre-assessment of your surroundings and resources, you can start thinking more specifically about what you're going to say. You probably have some butterflies in your stomach. It's normal to feel a mix of emotions right now. This is such an important conversation that you want to keep it *short and sweet* and give people time to digest the information you've given them. Setting a time limit is also a good strategy that gives *you* an "out" if you need it, but this may be more challenging to do with your parents. Your conversation with them is one you don't want to rush or make them feel like you're springing a surprise on them and bailing. But if the conversation goes poorly, it helps to have a natural reason to end it by saying something like, "I have to go to band practice right now. Can we talk about this again on Saturday?"

Everyone is different and this means that your coming out conversation will be different, depending on your relationship to them. The way you talk about your trans identity to your family, especially your parents, will likely differ from what you tell your friends, teachers and employer. You'll want the conversation to go as smoothly as possible, which means you'll need to think about how much detail you should give people and where you tell them. Here are some helpful suggestions for planning your coming out conversation.

Make a list of the people you want to come out to.

Start with the *safest* people who you know will likely accept you. Remember, it's important to build your confidence and get some practice to help you in conversations that will be more challenging. In addition, reaching out to the safest people helps you build a support network that you can fall back on for help and reassurance down the line. Chapter 4 goes into more detail about coming out to your friends.

Do your research.

When you first realized you were trans, you probably had a lot of questions about it. Well, anyone you come out to may feel similarly and are likely to know very little and have lots of questions. So be prepared with answers that can help them understand where you're coming from. Being knowledgeable also helps people see how serious you are about this and calm certain concerns or fears they may have. Consider printing out information you find from your research or getting pamphlets[6] from your local health center or guidance counselor to offer when you're coming out to people.

Research is more than facts. It's also about assessing your environments. You can try to "test the waters" of your family's or friends' reactions by bringing up a trans celebrity, a trans character on a television show, or a trans-related topic that's in the news—like a recent victory for trans rights. It's important to keep in mind that no matter how someone reacts to trans people who exist "out in the world," they can often have different feelings when the trans person is a friend or member of their own family.

Brace yourself to spend some time on this.

Being trans is not earth shattering—but it can feel that way to your family and friends. As frustrating or annoying as that may feel at times, people are allowed to have their feelings. That doesn't mean they're allowed to be *abusive* to you when they're expressing them, but it means that you can't expect everyone to immediately cheer for you. Coming out as trans is a life-changing event—both for you *and* for those who care about you—and some people will need time to adjust to the changes you're asking of them.

Expect *acceptance* to come with time. It may hurt to find that someone you love is having a hard time accepting who you are, but don't assume it's going to be this way forever. Remember: You've probably been thinking about your gender for years before you ever talked about it to someone else. It took you some time to adjust. It'll take them time too. Every person processes information differently. What you *can* do is provide them with accurate sources of information (which they may or may not choose to use), revisit the conversation when they feel more open to it, and give them space to digest the information you've given them. In the meantime, you can find solace and refuge with the people who are supportive of you.

While people are processing your new identity, it's perfectly fine to ask them to use the gender, name, and pronouns that you prefer. Indeed, doing so may help them make the mental shift faster. Just know though, it might take some time for them to adjust and you may have to remind them on occasion.

Don't set ultimatums, such as, "*Either you get on board with my transition or we'll never speak again.*"

Maybe such ultimatums will become necessary in the future, but give people time to see how they begin to process the information after the initial shock has worn off. If someone is being verbally or physically abusive though, it's best to put some distance between yourself and them for a while.

6 PFLAG and GLSEN

Consider time and place.

If you want people to consider your feelings, you have to consider theirs too. This includes choosing a time and place where they will be comfortable receiving your news. If you know this person well enough, choose a place that allows both of you to feel safe and one where you can easily leave if the conversation doesn't go well and you feel unsafe.

The key is to think about how they've reacted to surprising news in the past. If you have heard your parents make derogatory comments when listening to the news or say something mean in reference to another friend, this could be a sign that they may not be receptive to you at that time.

Practice what to say.

If you've ever been nervous about saying something out loud, like giving a presentation in front of class or asking someone on a date, you probably know how much practicing can help. Practice what you want to say. It will help you keep the conversation on track.

Whether it's using a mirror or just talking out loud to yourself, the more you practice, the easier it will be. Imagine yourself with the person and in the setting where you're going to tell them. Rehearse your opening lines and some of their possible reactions; then, have your back-up lines ready for their responses, including answers for questions you think they'll have.

Just do it.

Once you've made a list of people to tell and have a pretty good understanding of how they might react and feel like you're prepared, it's time to take action.

As I've already explained (above), going into the conversation feeling confident will take you a long way. People naturally respond more positively when they can sense your news isn't sad or scary to you. If you go into this with a positive attitude it's likely to rub off on others.

But everyone won't react well. No matter how much time and effort you put into planning, there is no guarantee that some people won't be surprised (and even shocked), confused, sad, or angry. That's why you need to have some back-up responses. Below are a few examples to consider. While these responses are in no way representative of how the people in your life will react, they are good possibilities and knowing them ahead of time may help you be more prepared.

You're wrong! You can't be trans.

You don't know what you're talking about.

You were born a girl (or a boy).

- "I *am* trans. I've thought about it for a long time and made sure I was certain before I decided to tell you."
- "Who I am can't possibly be wrong. It just *is*."
- "I've done a lot of thinking and research about this. Being trans means I don't feel like a boy (or a girl), and there are lots of people out there who are just like me."
- "How do *you* know your own gender? It's just something I feel inside."
- "I *do* know who I am, and I don't want to lie to you about it. I'd rather be open with you."

You're choosing to be this way.

Why can't you just decide to be normal?

- "I was born this way. It is not a choice."
- "This is *normal* for me."
- "I know you've probably never felt like your body was at odds with your gender, but mine just doesn't reflect the way I feel inside."

This is just a phase.

You'll regret this someday.

You're too young to know these things for sure.

- "I've been thinking about this for a long time."
- "I've done a lot of research and found there are many people who feel this way."
- "This is all I have been thinking about since I was _____ years old so I know it is not a phase."

You're just doing this for attention!

- "Why would I want to do that and have people bully me?"
- "I'm doing this for me and I'm telling you because I value our relationship and want you to know who I really am."

Why do you want to be this way? Life is going to be so hard for you now.

But you were always such a handsome boy (or pretty girl).

Now you won't be able to get married or have kids.

- "Life is hard for everyone, but my life will be less difficult if I can be who I really am."
- "Being a boy/girl wasn't right for me. This is the correct me."
- "Marriage equality is possible for me in most states nowadays. If I want kids, I also have options. There are medical procedures where I can have my eggs/sperm preserved for use at a later date. And I can always adopt children too, and there are many ways outside of that also."

Why are you doing this to me?

Everyone's going to blame me for this!

What am I supposed to do now?

- "This isn't about you. It's about me."
- "There's no one to 'blame' in this. Being trans isn't bad."
- "You're supposed to love me. Because I love you for all that you are."

People will have many questions for you, so decide ahead of time how much time you want to spend processing the new information with them and which questions you're willing (and not willing) to answer. Have some printed information available to give them if possible, including a list of sources they can go for further information about trans identities. *(See Appendices II, III, V.)* Educating people can help you maintain friendships and build allies. By giving people sources to learn more, you're making them feel included in your journey. Answer questions that you're only comfortable with. Be careful about venturing into areas that you're uncertain about. Just tell people that it's a sensitive area that you want to think more about before discussing it.

Sometimes people will react negatively to your coming out. If that happens, then tell the person that you'd like to talk at a later date when they're more emotionally settled. People are often more rational and calm after they've had a few days to process news. But if you think someone's emotions are likely to escalate into abuse, leave and get away from them. If you're in danger, find help immediately from a trusted adult like a teacher, counselor, family member, youth worker, or police officer. If you don't know where to turn, call a hotline for information on resources. *(See Appendix II for a list of resources.)*

Coming out to your parents.

Talking to your parents about being trans has its own unique considerations because of the special role they play in your life. Parents are often the people we worry about coming out to the most because we love them and want them to be proud of us. We may also be financially dependent on our parents. Because of these reasons and more, there are some important considerations to think about when telling them.

Consider your tone and volume.

Coming out is such an important conversation that you want to be conscious of your *tone of voice*. It's a big change for anyone, so be gentle with your parents. Revealing that you're trans is going to change the only reality of you that they've ever known, including all their dreams of how you were going to grow up and whom you were going to be. For example, fathers dream of walking their daughters down the aisle on their wedding day. Coming out to your parents will require them to shift their lives quite a bit. So be respectful and give them the same consideration you want them to give you.

When you begin talking, remember that people tend to mimic the tone that you set. It's a natural human response. So think about the tone you want your parents to use and start the conversation in that voice and volume. While this doesn't guarantee that your parents won't be shocked, one thing is for certain: If you start out in an angry or militant tone, you won't leave them any room to respond much differently. So speak in a calm voice.

Set a time limit (if you can).

When conversations drag on for too long, people get tired and emotionally exhausted. If you don't get to tell them everything you want in the first conversation, that's okay because there'll be other occasions to talk again. Try to end on a positive note if possible. That primes them to feel positive when you bring up the topic again.

Pick a time when your parents are more relaxed. For example: after dinner, a movie or television show, or a family outing like a bike ride or baseball game. Choose a time where you know it's best for them. Parents are busy and have stressful times where they're shifting gears from one thing to another like coming home from work and trying to make dinner or preparing the kids for school in the morning while thinking about getting to work on time. Avoid high-stress periods like these. Remember, the key is to make sure your parents are relaxed and not distracted by other things.

Telling your parents that you want to continue the conversation later sends a message that, while you've made some decisions for yourself that's independent of them, you still see (and want) them to be part of your transition and life.

Think through concrete goals.

Transition is a big change for parents. They need time to adjust to the news and changes that will be required of them. Try not to overload them with too much information in your first few conversations.[7] Instead, try to anticipate some of their reactions, especially their concerns or fears, and come up with responses you can say to ease their minds. (Refer back to the examples above.)

Go into the conversation with a clear purpose of what you want to cover and what you want your parents to get from it. (Example: *I'm going to let them know I've thought a lot about this, done my research, and that I know for certain that I'm trans.*) Make sure your goals are reasonable, too. It's unrealistic to expect your parents to understand everything about sex, gender identity, and sexuality in the first conversation. They will likely take longer to fathom the ways your body might change during a physical transition and will have many concerns about your medical health and physical safety.

One thing you can do to smooth over a rocky conversation is reassure your parents that you love them and that you are still the same person they've always loved and known. This can be conveyed by saying it aloud and/or, giving them a hug or holding their hand.

As much as you may be itching to cover more in the first conversation, it's better to give your parents a basic understanding of how you identify and offer those websites or information you printed, and then give them space to process. Hopefully, the materials will answer some of their questions. If your parents don't ask many questions, it's best not to overload them with information. In fact, I'd suggest staying away from the medical aspects (e.g., hormones) of gender reassignment in your first conversation, unless your parents insist on discussing it.

Start off strong and stay positive.

This is a big conversation, and while you might have a million things you want to tell your parents about being trans, you might not know how to *begin*. Here are some conversation starters that teens have used before:

---

7 Book for parents, Rex Butt, *"Now What? A Handbook for Families with Transgender Children"* (Transgress Press: Oakland, CA), 2015.

- *I want to share something important with you, and I just want you to listen, okay?*
- *I need to tell you something, and I hope you can keep an open mind.*
- *I need to talk to you about something, but I'm afraid you'll get worried.*
- *I want to be an honest person, so I'm going to share something with you.*
- *I've been keeping this in for a long time because I didn't know how to tell you before. I wasn't sure how you'd react.*
- *I've wanted to tell you for a long time now, but I love you and need you to know all of who I am.*

Listen as much as you talk.

Having a conversation, rather than just *telling* or *demanding*, means you also have to listen. This may seem like a hard thing to do, especially if your parents' reaction is different from what you were hoping. Remember that your parents are from another generation where gender transitions weren't talked about like today. As your parents they are concerned about your safety and health. They may be worried about what kind of a future you are going to have. They could be thinking that all the dreams they had of your future will have to change.

Genuine listening means tuning in and really trying to grasp not only what others are saying but *where* they're coming from and what your transition news sounds like from their *perspective*. After you've said what you needed to say, let your parents talk. When they're speaking, acknowledge that you're hearing what they say by keeping eye contact and nodding your head. Try to repeat back at least one point that they made to show them you are actively tuning in.

The bottom line: This is a conversation that you want to be respected in so you need to show respect, as well. Even if what your parents are saying doesn't sound or feel right, remember that it's not the end of your world. It's only their feelings, which can change over time. Affirming their feelings doesn't mean you're automatically negating your own. Nor does listening to them mean you're *agreeing* with them. You can help them digest your transition news easier and faster when you acknowledge their feelings and concerns. So listen calmly and resist the

temptation to get defensive. Someday you'll be old enough to make your own decisions, whether they're onboard or not.

Avoid a contest of wills.

Back-and-forth. Back-and-forth. That's the dynamic of a healthy conversation and *also* the description of a battle. Too easily, we can slide from the first to the second type. You don't want the conversation about your trans identity to grow into a contest of wills over who's right, who can yell the loudest, or last the longest. Nothing productive can come from that but misunderstanding, ill-will and estrangement. And just as bad, you're no closer to your transition goals.

When your parents express feelings that may be hard for you to hear, don't poke fun, snort at, or minimize their feelings. That's just *reacting*, which you want to avoid. Instead, you want to *respond*. What's the difference? Reacting is acting on your first emotions and snapping, jumping to judgment, laying blame, storming out, and raising your voice. Other things that jeopardize communication are: shouting, giving the silent treatment, pointing fingers, whining, turning to sarcasm, or threatening to run away. Responding, however, means stepping back to take a breath and thinking about how to move the conversation forward constructively. Sometimes, responding also means recognizing that the conversation should be tabled until a later time when cooler heads can prevail.

Lastly, I can tell you from experience, it's best to avoid speaking in the spirit of, "I'm right and you're wrong"—even *if* you know that's true. The stubbornness and anger behind this approach will show and turn your coming out conversation into a competition of wills that can escalate into an argument very quickly. Instead, approach your talk thinking, "We both will have our thoughts and opinions on this, and I simply need to make mine heard and hear theirs so I know how to move forward." *Try to put yourself in your parents' shoes and understand their point of view.*

Possible parental responses.

Remember too, your parents are capable of listening, being reasonable, and making decisions without becoming emotional. They may not be shocked at all. Because they have raised you, watched your behavior and listened to you for years, they may already have some inkling that you're trans. In any situation where people are dealing with loss (or potential loss), there are usually five emotions that they go through: denial, anger, bargaining, depression, and acceptance.[8] They don't necessarily go through these emotions in that order or go through all of them. But if they receive your coming out as a loss (or potential loss) they'll certainly exhibit some of these feelings.

The following are some examples of statements you might hear when they're experiencing these feelings. They may help you plan your response and prepare some answers beforehand.

DENIAL: Functions as a buffer or temporary defense after seeing or hearing shocking or unexpected news. It allows the parent time to collect themselves and possibly work toward acceptance.

- *This can't be true.*
- *You're wrong.*
- *It's just a phase.*
- *I blame your father (or the media, or your friends, etc.).*
- *I just can't deal with this right now.*
- *You can do whatever you want with your life once you're out of my house!*
- *I won't talk about that.*

Understand that when you hear these comments from your parents, while they may be in denial, they have heard you nonetheless. They could be building up a wall because the news may be overwhelming, even painful, for them. They may yell, cry, or give you the cold shoulder. But you must remember to remain calm and keep your emotions in check.

You should be prepared with some facts to respond:

- *Trans people are just born this way.*
- *It's not just a phase; it lasts for life.*
- *Nothing "causes" someone to be trans—not their environment or how they were raised.*

Your parents may feel they are to blame and that they did something wrong in your upbringing. Whether they have wondered about your gender identity or not, your coming out can still feel overwhelming to them.

ANGER: From your parents' viewpoint, the anger can be displaced because their life activities and dreams have become disrupted.

- *Don't talk to me anymore about it!*

8 *On Death and Dying*, Elizabeth Kubler-Ross..

- *Why are you doing this to us?*
- *I'm ashamed of you.*
- *Get away from me!*
- *You're ruining our family.*

While these things are difficult to hear. It's very important for you to let them speak. Keep your cool. **You had time to accept your trans identity and gather information for a long time, but your parents are hearing it for the first time.** They may say things that they'll apologize for later, so remain open to forgiving them if they want to make amends. Try to assess the situation at this point to see whether you can continue the conversation or wait a while and attempt to talk about it at another time.

BARGAINING: Sometimes people try to distract themselves from their feelings and the situation causing them. In your case, your trans identity and their shock/ fear and confusion. They may be unable yet to accept what you're saying and, in their best intentions, they may try to dissuade you.

- *Maybe you can change?*
- *I've neglected you; let's go shopping for clothes.*
- *If I let you cut your hair, will that be enough?*
- *If you get better grades, we will talk with you about this again.*

Be firm in your conviction about your trans identity.

DEPRESSION (CONFUSION AND GUILT): At this point, your parents may start asking themselves what they did *"wrong"* to *"cause"* this. They may be questioning how they raised you, or their own masculinity or femininity, their history as parents. That's heavy stuff, so be gentle. They may ask:

- *What did we do wrong to cause this?*
- *Why me/us?*
- *What am I going to do about this?*
- *What will people think? What will I tell them?*

People are going to have emotions and it's not your job to fix their feelings for them. You can't. No one can fix another person's emotional world. Everyone is responsible for their own feelings. If you're encountering responses like these from your parents, try introducing them to some of the research you've done. They may not know where to start, or feel too embarrassed to look up stuff, so have some websites or books ready to give them. Tell them about support groups like PFLAG. *(See Appendix II.)* Give them this book. It may help them understand.

Consider giving them space or finding new things to do together. They may be missing the things you used to do together. Be aware they're feeling like the past has been erased and may be depressed about that. You want to create new memories with them.

Strangely enough, it might seem for a while that you and your parents switch roles where they're learning from you rather than you learning from them. They may need you to give them space to express their feelings, and accept that they may make some mistakes while working towards understanding. You'll find that you have to repeat yourself sometimes, but don't become impatient.

Remind them you're the same person you always were, only better now that you're being honest about who you are.

Don't shut down. You can let them know, as nicely as possible, that it's a good thing you feel able to come to them with this. You need to keep the subject present, but be sensitive about it.

Understand that your parents want to feel loved and accepted by you just like you want that from them. They want to feel like you're still a family, even if some of the fantasies they had of your future are going to take a slightly differently path now. You may want to remind them of that. This will demonstrate your respect and sensitivity to their feelings. If you can take this approach to transition, you're more likely to get them onboard sooner than later.

It's critical that you use all of your listening skills. You can admit that you have some fears and worries too, but that you've done your soul-searching and your research, and you know that transitioning is the right thing for you.

ACCEPTANCE: Parents have attempted to work through the fact that you want to transition. There really is no time limit on this. It could be fairly immediate, or take years. Unfortunately, some parents may never get on board.

- *This isn't the end of the world.*
- *Let's make something good come out of this.*
- *I'm glad I understand you/your behavior better now.*
- *I'm willing to think about it. Let's make a plan.*

Remember, transitioning can be (and often is) a long journey. Realize that even though you want it to happen quickly, it will take time. And it may take your parents longer. If, by chance, the conversation doesn't go well at all, find someone else to confide in.

While I hope your parents and others will hear and accept you, I know things don't always turn out rosy. Remember your alligator skin and draw on your inner strength!

Your need and right to privacy.

You may want to control who knows about your trans identity and how it's explained to people and prefer to be the one who tells them. If this is so, I advise you to tell people that this is important to you and ask them to respect your privacy by not sharing your trans identity with others without first getting your consent. Tell them you want to come out on your own terms and in your own time. If they respect you, they'll keep your wish. This doesn't mean being trans is a "*secret*," it just means that it's your business of who to tell and when. As long as those people keep your trust, you might not feel like telling anyone else you're trans until you graduate high school or move out of your home. That's a valid option if it feels right for you.

Some benefits of coming out:

- It can be freeing; you won't have to keep living a lie.
- You can get the proper support needed.
- It could be easier to make LGBTQI friends.
- It may improve your self-esteem because you feel better about yourself.
- You will no longer be afraid of anyone finding out.

Some risks to be aware of:

- You could encounter transphobia or bullying.
- Your family and friends could treat you differently; or not talk to you.
- You could even lose friends.
- It is possible that you could get kicked out of your house and be homeless.
- You could lose the financial support of your parents.
- Or, they may feel uncomfortable around you.
- There may be an onslaught of personal questions.
- Many people may not be understanding.

When other people "out" you.

There could be a ton of reasons why someone would want to out you. It could be malicious to hurt you. Or, possibly a friend of yours may be thinking that they're being helpful to you. It is possible that another trans person may want to establish camaraderie with you by outing you. On the other hand, you could be outed accidentally in a conversation where someone may think that everyone knows. Whatever the situation, it's never okay for anyone to talk about your private business. It is yours to share only when you are ready.

However, you may find that your trans identity gets *"out of the box"* on occasion regardless of your careful planning. Sometimes a trusted friend slips up and starts talking about your transition without your permission or your parents find trans-related websites that you've visited in your Internet history.

When you're *outed*, it can bring up a lot of difficult emotions. You may feel shocked, betrayed, hurt, sad, scared, and anxious—kind of like a deer that's caught in headlights. You may also feel unsafe or receive a lot of positive, supportive attention, which can still be overwhelming in its own way. Being in the spotlight or under a microscope can feel uncomfortable, even overwhelming, at times. In contrast, some people can feel tremendous relief, because they don't have to put any more energy or time into deciding *who*, *when*, and *how* to come out. Whatever your emotions are, don't panic!

Calm down.

First, take a deep breath. Pause and take time to gather your thoughts. If possible, find a quiet place, turn off your phone and social media alerts, and let yourself think and feel. Write your thoughts and feelings down if it helps. If you have time later, maybe you can sit with a friend (perhaps another trans person) who will listen and comfort you. It may help to find something to distract your attention away from the situation for a little while, so you can relax and come back with a clearer mind.

Consider your next move.

Once you're past the initial "panic" phase, you can start assessing the situation and devising a plan for handling it. Your first question, as always, should be: *"Do I feel safe?"* Assess how people are reacting to the news and who might serve as a source of possible support as you move forward. Sometimes you can ask people who love you to be your ally. Also consider looking for support outside your circle of friends and family to youth groups, hotlines, or a counselor. Identify what *kind* of support you need in case you have to reach out to them.

HOTLINES If you need help reach out:
Trans LifeLine 1-877-565-8860
National Domestic Violence 1-800-799-7233
National Teen Dating Abuse 1-866-331-9474
GLBT National Youth Talkline 1-800-246-7743
Trevor Project 1-866-488-7386
National Runaway Safeline 1-800-RUNAWAY

Whether these situations describe you or not, you don't have to feel helpless or run away and hide. The world isn't coming to an end. You just need some tactics to help you deal with them when they arise. You could rehearse at home how to respond if someone outs you. Speaking calmly, say: *"You seem to have a lot of curiosity about me and that's interesting. If you want to know more about me, I'd be glad to tell you, but not now. Get back in touch with me later."* After that, *leave the situation*. Or, you may choose not to say anything. It is your right to respond as you see fit. In a situation like that, you will know what is best.

Basically, you want to regain control of as much of these conversations as you can by "setting people straight" about the realities of your identity before they start assuming, or telling stories, to help themselves deal with their own confusion or discomfort. Being confident and unashamed when you talk to people goes a long way towards them responding positively, and helping you feeling empowered.

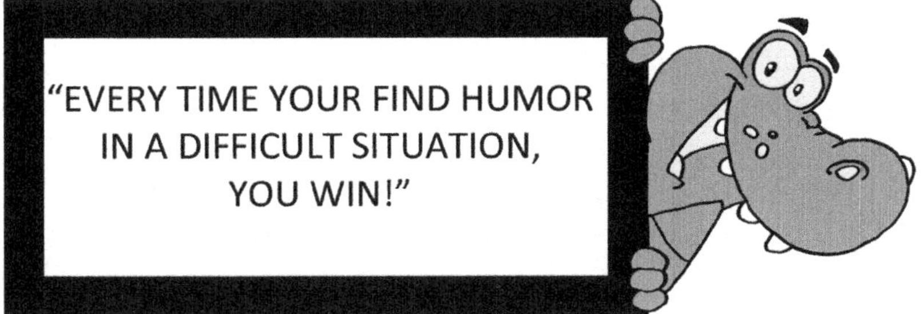

CHAPTER 3

Disclosure

Disclosure is similar to "coming out," but it's something that trans communities talk about more than gay, lesbian, and bi communities because trans people often face a more constant pressure to *tell* others about our personal history.

Many trans people choose to keep their trans history to themselves, telling only a few people they trust. There are a variety of reasons people don't disclose:

- They fear ridicule, bullying, harassment, and exclusion.
- They want to avoid invasive, inappropriate questions from others.
- They want to be recognized as the person they are rather than the gender that was wrong for them.
- They need to protect their families, careers and businesses.

After you've transitioned, or have begun the process, you'll encounter situations and instances throughout your life in which you'll have to think about whether you want to tell others about your trans history. There are many things to consider depending on the situation. —While others pressure trans people to think that disclosure isn't a choice or is something we should always do, you should remember that it's *your* choice to do so. Your body and life history belong to *you* and is yours to share when and where you want.

Our society makes the strange assumption that trans people have a *duty* to inform people of our identity and medical history. When people learn you're trans, sometimes, they'll pressure you with intimate questions about your childhood, romantic relationships—even your genitals—questions they would hesitate asking a cis-gender person. This is largely because the media sensationalizes trans peoples' lives and makes cis-gender people curious about us. There are some positive reasons to disclose your trans status, which I'll give some examples as we go along, but always remember that it's your decision.

Choosing whether to disclose your trans history is often about assessing how safe a situation is and weighing the potential problems that might arise as a result.

You may hear trans people talk of disclosure in scenarios like:

- *I met a new group of my friend's friends at the concert and chose not to disclose that I was trans.*
- *Did you decide to disclose your trans history to your date?*
- *The job application didn't ask about my trans status, but I chose to disclose it anyway.*
- *Someday, when I'm a parent, I think I'll disclose that I'm trans to my kids when they're young.*
- *We moved and have a new family physician now, and I'm trying to figure out how to tell her my medical history.*

While we could definitely insert "come out" into these sentences, using the word *"disclose"* helps us see how much talking about trans-ness pops up in all sorts of situations and can remain largely our *choice*—even if others think they can "tell" that we're trans. The importance of disclosure is because it's about respect of your privacy. Everyone's personal lives are deserving of equal respect. Because trans people are not well known or understood, people are uncomfortable and/or curious and don't always think before they ask questions. You never "owe it" to disclose your identity. You can use a situation as a teaching opportunity to remind them of personal boundaries.

It's a myth that we have to *"explain"* ourselves or share details about our past and our bodies. People's curiosity or discomfort doesn't mean that you have to carry a sign saying "Hi, I'm trans! Just thought you should know!" or automatically offer it up in conversations. We don't "owe" disclosure to anyone.

You may want to share your trans history with people as you get to know them better. It's inevitable when you become intimate or sexual with someone, but it's not a requirement for every person you meet. We'll talk more about dating and sex in Chapter 5 because these are special circumstances with their own unique pressures and challenges. When it comes to strangers or acquaintances, there are some questions and comments you don't need to answer. However, you should be prepared to respond.

When did you decide to become trans?

With this question, people may really be asking: "How or when did you realize you're trans?" You and I know that being trans isn't a choice. We're born this way. It's true that we choose when to begin transitioning, but for those of us who need to take medical steps, it's not a choice—it's *medically necessary*. *"Medically necessary"* means we need to transition in order to live, which means the choice is really, *"Do I want to live my life as the person I really am?"* The answer to this question for almost everyone, trans or not, is ***YES***.

What's your "REAL" name?

Your real name is the name that's right for you. Every trans person makes a decision about their name. Sometimes, it's simply keeping one's birth name. However, many trans people select a new name for themselves that feels more genuine. When people imply that a *birth name* is more real than a *preferred* or *chosen name*, they may be questioning the authenticity of a trans person's entire gender and identity. You are real because you know and say who you are—just like everyone else.

Are you sure you aren't gay?

As I explained in the previous chapter, sexual orientation and gender identity are two separate things. This question usually comes from people's confusion of trans identities with lesbian, gay and bisexual identities. Everyone has both a gender, and sexual orientation. Being trans and being gay—or lesbian, bisexual, or queer—cannot, by definition, *be* the same thing. Trans refers to the gender you *identify as* while sexuality refers the gender you're *attracted* to. Of course, you may be both trans and gay, lesbian, or bisexual. The key is to remember they're separate traits coexisting side-by-side. So, it's not a matter of whether you're trans *or* gay, but that you're trans *and* may also be gay or bisexual or heterosexual.

Wow! You look so "normal." I would have never known you are trans!

People often believe that trans people want nothing more than to blend[9] into "normal" society. There *is* no such thing as "normal." Everyone has their own gender identity, and the way they express it. There are more traditional ways of "looking like" a man or woman, and many trans people do indeed want to *"blend"* into mainstream society at certain times.

9 A term I use—rather than the word "pass". It means that you are one of the crowd and recognized as your true self.

The problem with this statement isn't so much its assumption that trans people want to blend in with everyone else, as the presumption that trans people stick out visibly and everyone can always tell we are trans. This assumption is wrong. There's nothing shameful about being trans. Whether others can identify your trans identity or not doesn't mean that you or your transition are a failure.

Have you had "THE Surgery"?

People love asking trans people about the physical transformations we've made to our bodies and this is very invasive. Sometimes, people will probe further and ask about your genitalia. Why is this a problem? Again, because talking about our bodies is a very intimate topic and most people don't ask cis-gender people to talk about their bodies, especially their genitalia. You can politely decline by saying, "That's a pretty intimate topic and I only have those discussions with my physician (or my partner or people I date)." Or you could say: "That's a very personal question which I'm not inclined to discuss details." The answer I give in a very polite tone is, "Why would you ask something like that?" It then puts the question to the person who is asking. Remember too, that being trans isn't defined exclusively by or reduced to whether you've had surgery or hormones or changed your legal identification or wear certain clothes, etc. You're trans (or whatever gender identity you prefer) because you *say you are.*

How do you have sex?

This question is closely related to the surgery question and is similarly invasive and rude, but you will undoubtedly encounter it at least once in your lifetime. It's amazing how quickly people's curiosity leads them to forget basic rules of social interaction, especially when it comes to respecting trans people's privacy. Personal questions about your genitals, sex life, even those like, "*What bathroom do you use?*", or "*How do you go to the bathroom?*" can be off-putting. Remember your private parts are just that—*private.* To politely deflect this line of questioning, you could say, "I use the restroom like everyone else" or turn it around by asking: "Don't you think that's a little personal to ask someone?"

What did you look like before you transitioned?

People think *a lot* about bodies: their own and others. A person's body is the first thing we notice about them, and we make all sorts of unconscious assumptions and assessments about "who" a person is based simply on what they look like. This applies whether you're trans or not, and you and I do it too.

When someone knows you've transitioned, or have taken steps to change your appearance, they can become fixated on wanting to know what you looked like in the past. This may feel like they're invalidating your true gender, and it's really none of their business. Like any of these questions or comments, it's not something you have to answer.

Again, if someone asks or says something that makes you feel uncomfortable, *trust your intuition and listen to your gut instincts.* You have the right to privacy and to have your gender and history respected, and that includes maintaining boundaries with what people can and cannot ask you. To these inappropriate or uncomfortable questions, you can simply say:

- *That's private.*
- *I'd rather not talk about it.*
- *That's not something I really talk about with other people.*
- *I know this is a little awkward, but I'd rather talk about something else.*
- *I haven't really thought about that yet.*
- *Why would you ask that?*

Or, you can ignore their question by simply moving on to another topic without acknowledging at all. If they tuned in to your redirection of the conversation, they'll key in to your discomfort and make the shift. They may even apologize for their lack of forethought.

If you are with a friend who understands, you can talk to them ahead of time and ask them to intervene on your behalf. If you're in a conversation with someone new who brings up one of these questions, your friend can help you by taking the attention off you or bringing up a new subject.

If you feel like your new acquaintance might respond poorly to you, re-direct the conversation to what you need to do to feel safe. **Being safe is the first priority**. Know that making the decision to *come out* or *disclose* your trans identity or history doesn't mean you have to be open to satisfy people's curiosity. ***Your transition isn't public property***.

CHAPTER 4

School, Friends, and Bullying

School.

Whether you like it or not, unless you're homeschooled, you can't avoid school if you decide to medically transition. Going to school and doing your best to excel is essential to your development as a person, a good citizen, and your ability to be successful and contribute to society.

Schools are increasingly becoming a *"safe space"* for trans students as more are adopting policies that protect and support gender diversity. Since you spend a large chunk of your waking hours in school, it's also worth locating some allies, specifically, a person or people on whom you can depend.

So, what's your school like? Is it a safe place to come out? Ask yourself:

- *Do I get a general sense that "difference" is acceptable?*
- *Have other kids come out as LGBTQI? How did it go?*
- *Who would be safe to come out to?*
- *Who would I be comfortable coming out to?*
- *How will I handle negative reactions, if I encounter them?*
- *Is there a way to formally report and address bullying if it occurs?*

If you can answer **"Yes"** to all these questions, you're in a great place! Some schools are liberal and have progressive policies regarding trans rights, but many schools aren't and students and staff can put pressures on teens to conform to traditional notions of "woman" and "man." While you can still come out in a setting like this, remember that your number one priority is *your* safety. It could be that your safest option is to come out after you finish high school. It's not that you shouldn't live your life openly and proudly as whom you are, but you should be aware that some school situations are not so black and white. Simply surviving until you can graduate may be the only right choice you can make at this moment in your transition. However, if you feel safe, then I suggest rehearsing a few lines that you can say when someone outs or attempts to out you. This way you are prepared with a thoughtful response when it happens. Outing is a form of bullying. If they are mean, the idea is to defuse them by being nice.

Coming out may occupy so much of your mind for a while that you can forget why you're in school: to learn knowledge and build academic and social skills. The sooner you find a safe haven in your school environment, the quicker you can refocus your energies on school, which will also help you feel balanced and emotionally stable. You may feel like coming out has thrown everything around you into chaos, so it's probably in your best interest to wait out the high emotions and drama.

Coming out at school: thinking it through.

Change never happens if someone isn't the "first" to do something new. Some trans students feel comfortable and capable of taking on harassment or rejection to make a statement about their right to transition. Other students attend a school where being trans would hardly cause a ripple. We naturally pick up on the "temperature" of our environments simply by observing how *"difference"* is treated—not just in regards to gender, but other identities also, like sexual orientation, race, ethnicity, religion, nationality, language, and more.

While you can never be 100% sure of people's responses before you come out, if you feel like it's time to start telling people at school, the first step is the same as coming out to your family: *Plan ahead.*

Testing the waters.

Before you announce that you're trans to other students try to gauge their responses using some strategies like mentioning a trans news story or television character in conversation to check out people's reactions. If you don't want to jump immediately into discussing trans people, you can try bringing up gay, lesbian, or bisexual celebrities or stories. Keep in mind, though, that people sometimes respond differently to differences in sexuality than they do to gender. As marriage equality is now legal across the US and gays and lesbians are becoming more in the mainstream, society is becoming increasingly acceptable of LGB people. But, in some of these same spaces, transphobia may still be acceptable because trans people haven't made the same gains as the lesbian and gay movement. So take your time when testing the social atmosphere for trans acceptance.

Finding your allies.

Have you felt comfortable talking with a particular guidance counselor, teacher, or coach and felt that they might be open to you? Maybe your school has a Gay/Straight Alliance that can provide you with built-in peers and teachers who will support you. Make a list of your allies ahead of time. Remember, as we discussed in Chapter 2, first come out to people who you are more certain will react with support so you can get some practice and build allies.

Bracing yourself for potentially negative reactions.

Fear and discomfort with gender diversity is so pervasive in our society that it's almost inevitable that at least *one* person in your school will express disbelief, anger, or even disgust when you come out as trans. Ideally, they're in the minority and you have your allies to back you up and reinforce the idea that transition is just a part of life. Perhaps you've tested the waters and have gotten the sense that a negative response will be strong, but you've still decided it's worth it to feel liberated.

This is the point where you imagine "worst case scenarios," and ask yourself what you'd do in such situations. What if you were teased in the hall? Threatened with violence? Mis-gendered by teachers and classmates who ignored your requests for correct pronouns? You must be prepared for these situations, so that you can have a strategic response. If things like this happen, is there an administrator who can help you deal with it? Or is it best for you to take your worries to a parent, family member, friend or other trusted adult who can advocate for you?

Let's talk through some of the safe people and spaces that could provide you with shelter.

Coming out to a friend.

Friends are often the first people trans teens come out to. Sometimes, our peers understand us in ways that parents and teachers don't, so it makes sense that you think they might have the best reaction. If you come out to a friend first and the experience goes well, you'll have some practice and support for when you come out to your parents, classmates, or teachers.

Of course, friends can have all sorts of responses—some may be supportive and others might feel confused or upset. They may wonder why you didn't tell them sooner, or feel like they hardly know you anymore. Friendships often hold some of our most intense emotions, and you could encounter some unexpected turbulence. Just like with coming out to your parents, it's worth taking a little time to think through how you'll come out to your friends. Here are some tips to keep in mind:

- *Pick a friend who is most likely to respect you by not talking about you behind your back.*
- *Have a back-up plan if things go poorly: a parent, sibling, or trusted adult who you can turn to for advice and support.*
- *Know that friends, like parents, take time to process news. You still have to be patient with them.*
- *Expect your friendship to change—often for the better (you become closer) or possibly for the worse (you grow distant).*

The funny thing about friends is whenever you tell them something new about yourself, sometimes they receive it as a personal reference on themselves, wondering, "*What does this mean about ME?*" It's something we all naturally do—you and I have done this too—because peers, in some sense, are our "mirrors." We observe their actions, new outfits or looks they try on, and their mistakes and successes as a way of learning about ourselves.

Knowing this can help you understand explain some of your friend's responses. One of their first thoughts may be, "*What does this mean about MY gender?*" Perhaps they've never thought deeply before about how society forces gender roles on us or they've never considered the reality that not everyone identifies with the sex they were assigned at birth. When you come out as trans, they may not understand what that means. That doesn't change the fact that your gender is *real*, but it does mean that friends might pull away because they may not understand at first and need time to think more. They might initially deny or refuse to accept your new reality, or they might probe with a ton of curious questions.

It's important to recall here, the invasive questions we discussed in Chapter 3. Even if they're your friend, you still don't have to give in to their pressured to talk about your body or identity in ways that make you feel uncomfortable. Friends should respect your privacy.

The second thing a friend may wonder after you come out is, "*What does this mean about our friendship?*" Since figuring out you're trans has, in some sense, meant not sharing your "whole" self with others, sometimes friends interpret this as, "You were keeping a secret from me." The reality, of course, is that you needed time to figure out exactly what you wanted to say before you started talking about it, but that doesn't keep close friends from feeling hurt sometimes. That's something, that they need to work through on their own—you don't "owe" it to them to share everything about yourself before you're ready, and it's not your responsibility to process their feelings for them.

Sometimes friendships can't withstand these issues, and they fall apart—but that's an extreme case. If some friends can't handle your trans identity, as hard as it may seem, you will have to move on from those friendships and make new ones. Most often, friends just need time to adjust to the new parameters of your friendship. They need time to adjust to your new name and pronouns. Even if they're upset at first, most friends appreciate when we are honest with them. Friends feel honored when we call upon them for support in facing parents, teachers, or school bullies. Friends generally stick by us because that's how real friendships work.

Coming out to a teacher or counselor.

Adults at school hold a special place in our lives: They're not parents, yet they're responsible for elements of our safety and well-being. Most students have at least one teacher or guidance counselor with whom they've bonded, and experience feelings of caring and trust. They're primed to be our advocates or "go-betweens" when it comes to parents or school administrators. As a general rule, teachers work in the field of education because they care about young people and want you to be healthy and safe.

Keep in mind that teachers are humans, though. They can have a range of reactions. At the risk of sounding like a broken record, I'll reiterate again: Plan ahead for unexpected or negative responses. The great thing about teachers is they can be a safe, parent-like adult for you, but because of their role in your life, they're less likely to react as strongly as your parents might. They are a safe way to "practice" coming out to other adults, and they can be your support as you come out in more difficult spaces.

Teachers are also employees of the school, which means that they face pressures from administrators to enforce school standards. If a school's environment and leadership is transphobic, even supportive teachers may feel they cannot vocalize their support of your transition. They may let you know in a more subtle way however, by allowing you to sit after school in their room (providing a "safe space"), being proactive about squashing any gender-based teasing they hear, or steering you towards other adults who are more able to help you. Look for a "Safe Space" sticker from GLSEN[10] that supportive adults often post on their classroom door.

10 http://www.glsen.org/

If your school has a Gay/Straight Alliance, it's worth seeing if you can talk to that teacher. They've made it known publically to the school body that they're comfortable with LGBTQI students, so they may be the best adults to support you. Guidance counselors are hired specifically to talk with teens about challenges or changes in their lives. Again, you may want to "test the waters" by bringing up a trans topic with them before you say, "I'm trans," since some counselors are transphobic. If a counselor feels safe to you, they may help you work through difficult emotions better than a friend. Many counselors are required to keep your conversation "confidential," meaning they can't tell anyone about it, unless you're at risk for harming yourself or someone else.

Beyond your safe space: coming out to classmates.

Coming out to everyone at your school about your trans identity may feel daunting. School can be hard enough with social groups and popularity contests, homework deadlines, and the extracurricular responsibilities of clubs or sports. Throw puberty and hormones into the mix, and people's moods and actions seem all but impossible to predict. Yet, it can feel downright *necessary* to be out at school—hearing the wrong pronouns and name day-in and day-out can often weigh on you over time. So, coming out regardless of people's responses, may feel liberating.

Sometimes, we can come out to classmates in one big move: At a school assembly for a Diversity Day, in a school newspaper, or even on the school "news" program or Facebook. But more often, people come out to classmates on an individual basis by word-of-mouth.

Once the cat's out of the bag, it may feel like a thousand eyes are on you.

Being out can be energizing. You're feeling whole, authentic, and proud, and you're making life *a little easier* for other trans students coming up behind you. If your friends have your back, it probably feels like you can take anything that comes your way—even teasing or ignorance. You'll quickly realize that at some point however that you're going to meet some haters who just can't wrap their mind around your transition.

School bathrooms, sports, and locker rooms.

As part of transitioning in school, you (and possibly your parents) will have a conversation to discuss which bathroom to use. You should be aware of the fact that you *can* use the bathroom that aligns with your gender identity. Whether the teacher's bathroom or nurse's bathroom is available, you should only use those bathrooms if it is *your* choice. It is possible that you may hear other things such as, safety, or the parent of another student feels that your choice is inappropriate. The reality though is that, these issues have nothing to do with you. Nor are they your responsibility; they are for the school administrators to handle. They have nothing to do with you. TITLE IX[11] protects your right to use the locker room and sports team of your choice. It may be a matter of getting the school on board (and possibly educated). Something to remember: It is always good to have an ally (friend) who can go with you into the locker room for emotional support. Knowing that your friend is with you, adds to your inner strength and ability to cross that barrier for the first time.

Facing your haters.

When people are uncomfortable or confused, sometimes they lash out at the source—in this case, you! This might come in the form of shouting insults in the hallway, intimidating you online, making jokes about LGBTQI people, trying to shame you in front of others, taking or damaging your belongings, or even trying to shove or hit you. Often, this stuff is done behind closed doors and away from those who would usually intervene.

One of the most important things to keep in mind, too, is that whoever or whatever is harassing you, it won't go on forever. It's only temporary and there are solutions. When you're in the midst of being badgered, it can feel like the situation will continue forever. The reason for this is because we mistake the *intensity* of our feelings for the *reality* of the situation and forget that it will change eventually. Put a different way, sometimes our feelings of hurt, fear, anger, and sadness can be so overwhelming in the moment that we forget to think rationally that:

- *I'm not going to be at this school forever;*
- *I'm going to graduate one day and get away from here;*
- *They are not the only teachers/students. I can make friends with others.*

Obviously, these things are true, but you can forget them when you're in the throes of hardship. So remember that when you're feeling down in the dumps, it's not forever. You're destined for something bigger and better.

So, what's a trans teen like you to do? Let's do some thinking. From experience, I've found it's best to try to assess what's behind these situations. Here are some things to consider:

11 TITLE IX https://www.aclu.org/blog/victory-title-ix-protects-transgender-students
http://www.justice.gov/crt/about/cor/coord/titleix.php
http://www2.ed.gov/about/offices/list/ocr/docs/qa-201404-title-ix.pdf
If the school receives any federal money—almost every school does—they must abide by the rules of TITLE IX!

You're not alone.

Many trans people who came before you have been in your shoes and walked a similar path, some of whom you have probably read about: Jazz Jennings, Laverne Cox, and Chaz Bono, for example. Even at this moment, there are a growing number of trans teens in your *exact same position*. It's comforting to know that you aren't the only one going through this experience, and it could be helpful for you to try to find some of those other teens to talk to. It's also helpful to find stories of trans adults who have successfully navigated their teen years, and have come out happy and strong on the other side.

"An eye for an eye leaves the whole world blind."[12]

Hitting back at those who've hit you may seem like the most logical step. Someone calls you a name? You call them a worse one. Someone makes a joke about your clothes? You tease them in front of all their friends. Someone trips you when you're walking down the hallway? You push them into a wall the next time you see them.

Reacting to anger with anger or violence is not the proper solution and the consequences are almost always bad. Immediately tell a trusted adult if someone harasses, intimidates, or bullies you. Being mean to or angry with other people only leaves you feeling bad inside. It can even make us into bullies when we encounter more vulnerable people in other spaces. Your primary value is to help promote acceptance of people's differences and violence only undermines that.

Compassion can make a world of difference.

One of the best ways to deal with attackers is to try to understand *why* they feel the need to hurt others. Bullies often target people who they see as *"different"* or vulnerable because they themselves feel small inside. This could be because they've been hurt by others at some point in their lives or because they've inherited a small worldview from their families that doesn't encompass gender diversity. When they're afraid, they look for someone else to hurt as a temporary fix, and they may see you as an easy target or victim because you're so visibly different. This doesn't condone their actions *at all*, but it does give you some insight on their behavior, and helps you realize: *There's nothing wrong with you, because the bullying is really about them.* They are trying to show their power over you. This is the time to show the power of your own alligator skin and how you won't be pulled down to their level, even though it seems difficult at first. Each day you resist giving in, you grow stronger.

12 M.K. Gandhi.

Taking action.

Having compassion for and not reacting to bullies *doesn't* mean that you shouldn't fight back or protect yourself. You're not a doormat. But understanding the psychology of bullying makes it clearer that the best way to fight is not with your fists or nasty words. Using your maturity and reason instead, you can walk away from situations calmly, rather than escalate them. Here's how:

Take a deep breath.

Just like we discussed in Chapter 2 about talking with your parents, avoiding conflict with classmates or other bullies is best done from a clear-headed mental place. This means pressing the *"pause"* button the moment you hear an insult or joke so that you can *respond from a place of strength rather than react from a place of anger or fear*. Humans are built with a **"fight or flight"** instinct that kicks in whenever we're threatened. Your initial **"fight"** impulse may be to lash back—but that's an ineffective way to deal with bullies.

Defuse the bomb.

A heated exchange with a bully is a recipe for explosion. If you stay chill and quiet, their rage has no fuel to grow on. If a bully yells, don't yell back. Just keep talking in a normal tone. I call this *"defusing the bomb."* If you think about bomb squads on television shows, how do they act? *Calm and collected*. They're in control of themselves. That's exactly how you should act around a loud, angry, or violent situation. If you don't yell or hit back, their actions are less likely to escalate and turn into something more.

Assert your right to be yourself.

You and I both know there's nothing wrong with being trans. Let the bullies know—then let it go. *Their ignorance is their problem to solve, not yours*. You don't owe it to anyone to be their educator. You're just here to live your life and let others live theirs. You can stand up for yourself by letting them know, while keeping your emotions in check, that you're still going to be yourself and they should just find someone else to go bother.

Walk away.

The minute you sense someone else escalating the situation, this should be a sign for you to walk away. This can feel hard at first. If you don't snap and react to a bully's put-down, it may seem like you're letting them "get away with it." It might even feel like you're saying: *It's okay to pick on trans people.* That's not really what you're doing. Rather, you're telling them several things:

- *What you have to say doesn't matter.*
- *I will not be your victim.*
- *I value my time and myself more than your insults.*
-

Whether bullies interpret it this way or not, they're less likely to attack you again if they know they can't get a "rise" out of you or win. Further, our hearts hear the message even when the bullies don't and our confidence and feelings of self-worth are bolstered whenever we take an action that says, "*I'm better than this.*"

Talk to an ally.

Bullying can be emotionally exhausting too. Even when we get good at standing up for ourselves, it's tiring to know that we have to keep doing this. One way to counter feelings of fatigue and frustration, especially if bullying continues or new bullies arise, is to find someone to talk to. Sharing our struggles with a trusted ally can boost our energy to keep forging ahead. If your friends are aware of what's going on, they may even stand by your side the next time your attacker comes around. Bullies most often feel powerful when you're alone and isolated from friends. Having a group of friends around strengthens you.

Consider getting school teachers and administrators involved.

Sometimes, the best way to deal with a situation is to get teachers, counselors, or administrators involved. This is up to you. Most of us can sense when a situation is something we can handle. If you're at the point where you are wondering, "*Is this bullying*?", the answer is: ***Yes***. Trust your gut. Taking more formal action against your attackers is not a sign of "weakness," "tattle-tailing," or "copping out." Rather, it's claiming that you're a valuable person whose freedom and life matter and are worth protecting.

Most schools have policies against bullying and harassment, and some have proactive programs for making the school a "Safe Space." You may find information in your school handbook about how to find these safe spaces and deal with bullying. If you do not have a school handbook, or need help finding information, ask a parent, an outside adult, or a friend to go with you to you talk to an administrator about what's been going on. Be sure to keep notes of when, where, and how the bullying happened, so that you'll be better prepared to make your "case."

Sometimes, a school administration is unaccepting or resistant to trans people and our rights. If you've complained about bullying, and the school isn't taking action, this is the time to consider going above them to file a formal complaint. If you feel comfortable, you can approach your school district's superintendent. Set up a meeting to talk about the bullying, how you've asked your school to address it, and how long it's continued. Make sure you bring a list of the teachers and administrators who've neglected to help you. School districts are scrutinized by your state government and the media too sometimes, so some school administrations are proactive about defusing bullying situations before they get worse.

Internet/social media.

When it comes to Facebook, Instagram, Tumblr and any other media hot spot, you need to remember one of your tools that we talked about earlier. Like most things in life, you have a choice. The choice in this situation is to ignore what they say. If the comment is on Facebook then block, unfollow or unfriend them. Do not become their victim. Unless you have mistreated someone their opinion of you should not matter. One of the things you can say to yourself when someone is not nice, or they are being opinionated about you is, "your opinion of me is none of my business" (Richard Flint lecture). Take anyone of your favorite musicians or actors. If you listen to any of them talk about social media, they are well aware that there are many nasty and horrible comments made about them. They will also tell you that they don't waste time reading those comments and neither should you! So, consider following their example because you can't control other people's behavior. You can only control your own.

Whatever you do, stay in school!

No matter how difficult things may feel at times, don't drop out! It may seem like the easiest way to relieve pressure from your life when other problems are popping up, but your education isn't the thing to sacrifice to feel relief. If you're stressed out, look elsewhere for solutions. Keep walking away from those bullies, invest less time with people who aren't supportive, and/or get exercise. Try whatever works, that's not harmful to your health, to get you to the finish line.

I know it's hard to think years into the future, but one thing is certain: Your life *will be much harder without a diploma*. This is true for everyone, trans or not. Dropping out limits your job opportunities and makes it almost impossible to realize your dreams. Completing your transition is probably one of your dreams, but without a job, it is extremely difficult to transition fully. What is more, your life will likely be hampered more by a low paying job as opposed to one that lets you live the life you want. Don't let bullies take your future away from you.

It's a fact that facing constant hardship can affect one's ability to succeed in school. It can lead to sadness and depression, which can take away our interest in school, sports or activities, even if we used to enjoy them. So check in with yourself right now.

- *Are you missing classes to avoid bullies or people's stares?*
- *Do you feel **"out of it"** or think, **"I don't care"** when you think about schoolwork?*
- *Do you feel so down that you can't imagine yourself getting your dream job or going to college anymore?*

If you answered **"Yes"** to any of these that means that external factors are affecting your ability to focus on your work, and preventing you from succeeding and making a future for yourself. You have the power to get back on track. The first step is to recognize if you've fallen into a pattern of avoiding schoolwork, or seem to be living in a mental "fog." If you determine that being bullied or the stress of coming out is affecting your schoolwork, here's what to do.

- *Talk it out with someone—a teacher, coach or guidance counselor—who you trust.*
- *Consider asking if you can talk to a therapist. Asking for a therapist shows your maturity and commitment to self-care.*

At the end of the day, *it is your life* and you have to take responsibility for yourself. There are many means of support out there. Sometimes it only takes one person to help you!

CHAPTER 5

Dating and Relationships

When I talk to trans teens, one of the things they want to talk about is dating. This makes sense. You're young. You've come to terms with the reality of your gender identity and quite naturally you want to explore your sexuality too. Dating brings up all those questions about disclosing your trans identity to someone else which we discussed in Chapter 3, not to mention the butterflies that bounce in your stomach when you're crushing on someone.

Above all else, remember that dating should be fun. It's also about finding another person who loves and sees you as you are. Sometimes, this can be complex for trans people. We get a lot of messages from the larger world that we are unlovable or unattractive simply because we have identities and bodies which people aren't always familiar with. Don't settle for someone who you're not attracted to, or who doesn't treat you right, simply because you think no one will date you because you're trans.

Always remember this: You are beautiful and worthy of love and respect.

There are plenty of people in the world who will be attracted to you and want to date you because they like and want to get to know *you* as a person. Eventually, you will find the right person or people, and you can do some of the legwork necessary for relationships long before you ever start swimming in the dating pool. It's okay, too, if you don't feel like dating. Not everyone does, and dating is not a necessary way to validate who you are, but it feels nice when other people are attracted to us.

Loving yourself first.

It might sound like a cliché, but it's true: *You cannot love someone else and have a healthy relationship, if you don't love yourself first.* The energy and authenticity that's required to be in a truly loving relationship starts with *you.*

Ask yourself:

- *Do I have a firm sense of "who I am?"*
- *Do I like myself? Love myself?*
- *Do I like the person I'm becoming?*
-

The reason you should explore these questions before dating someone is because **dating often puts pressure on us to meet someone else's ideals**—their picture of who we "should" be. If you don't have a strong sense of self, it's easy to lose yourself—or sense of who you are—in a relationship.

For example, if you date someone who likes you because of the dresses and make-up you wear, you might feel like you have to wear dresses and make-up all the time, even if you want to occasionally deviate from that style. Or your date finds your muscles sexy. Your main reason for working out may simply be to stay in good physical shape, but you may find yourself doing more exercise and trying dietary supplements in an attempt to maintain their attraction to you.

These things can happen to any anyone, but being trans can weigh *extra* heavily on our reason for staying in a relationship that's not good for us, because we may feel *extra* vulnerable to rejection and assume that no one else will love us. Understanding and handling rejection is part of dating and life. Adolescents are experimenting with who they are, who they are with, what they like and what they don't like; and trying to build their self-confidence by finding out more about themselves. It is just another experience to propel you forward. Allow yourself a moment of sadness or hurt and then move on to a better you. In the end, remember these two things: 1) there are more people who will love you for yourself; and 2) it's rare for people to find their soulmate or life partner at your age.

Even if our bodies and genders are not the "norm," that doesn't mean they're not beautiful and lovable.

Before you date, take some time to form a healthy self-image. When you feel poorly about yourself, when you feel ashamed, you only attract people who put you down and make you feel worse. What can you do today to love yourself? Smile in the mirror? Put on an outfit that makes you feel good? Listen to your favorite band? Go for it.

Keeping balanced.

Dating can be a wonderful experience. It's a way to learn more about yourself, what you like in another person, and what turns you off. Dating can be a big part of being a teen and figuring out the adult you're becoming.

When you get really excited about a relationship, it's easy to put your schoolwork, family life, and hobbies aside. The teens I've talked to have been happy dating people who were also attracted to them. Sometimes, they even fell in love. Some of them got into steady relationships with their new partner, and began to have, or considered having, sex. The emotions around all of these things are *huge*, and at times these teens became distracted from focusing on schoolwork or other relationships with friends, siblings, or parents. Remember to keep your eyes on the big picture, and maintain a heathy balance with other areas of your life: school; your self-care (including your transition); and your future. These are important for your long-term success and happiness in life, whether you're partnered in a relationship or not.

Don't define yourself through your partner.

What does this mean? Don't forget yourself, your ambitions and values. Make time for your own needs and wants, like your hobbies, studying hard to get good grades, and spending time with friends and family. It means not dropping what you're doing the minute your partner calls. It means that if your happiness or sadness is dependent on your partner's approval or presence in your life, then you need to take a step back and think about what you like about yourself and your life that's important to you and make sure you communicate it to the person you're dating.

Disclosure.

We touched upon this issue in the chapter on disclosure, but we need to go over it again here. One of the most common things trans teens wonder about is *if*, *when*, and *how* to tell someone they're dating that they're trans. Again, the answer is there's no one right or wrong way to do it. It's all about who you are as an individual and what feels most comfortable for you.

You have the right to choose how to discuss your own gender identity and body. Other people may try to convince you otherwise, but that doesn't change this fact. *You don't owe anyone an explanation for being you.*

Many consider their trans identity to be private information and choose not to talk about it on the first date or two. Other people mention it upfront before they go on a date to avoid wasting their time with someone who isn't accepting. Maybe for you, you'll feel like mentioning it after hanging out a few times because you feel like the relationship may lead to something more serious or lasting.

Whatever your situation, you need to feel comfortable with that person. Sometimes delaying disclosure can make you feel more anxious knowing that you have something to say. **The key is to remember your safety**.

As we discussed in the previous chapter, being trans is not a big secret that you should feel like you're "hiding" from someone. The reality of our world is that you also have to be cautious about when, where, and to whom, you disclose your identity. This might make some people you date feel as though you were "keeping a secret" from them and "lying by omission". These reactions largely come from a society that misinforms us that trans people are being deceptive, when in reality we're simply being careful and protecting ourselves against unpredictable (and sometimes harmful) reactions when we disclose our history.

If your date reacts unpleasantly or surprised by your disclosure, things could turn uncomfortable, awkward, or even dangerous. This is why some trans teens choose to have the conversation with their date *earlier* rather than *later*, especially before getting physical or having sex.

Just like coming out conversations, disclosing your trans identity to a potential partner is best done while both of you are in a calm non-sexual space. *Don't wait until you're in the heat of sexual passion to disclose.* And if you fear an adverse reaction or can't confidently predict it will go smoothly, you should consider having the discussion in a public space, like a cafe or restaurant.

You may be totally smitten with your crush, but sometimes people can't handle finding out that you're trans. If you disclose and your date gets upset and the situation escalates in the wrong way, you should get out of that situation and move on. If you're on a date and it goes badly after you've disclosed, then leave, or call or text a friend. In fact, tell several people beforehand, where you're going on your date, in case things don't go as planned and you need some backup.

After you have disclosed to your date that you are trans, you may find that your relationship is advancing toward something more sexually intimate. If you know that there is a chance for a sexual encounter, it is best to have a discussion first before waiting until you're in a sexual situation. Usually conversations about sex are best held in a non-sexual atmosphere. Communicate and share your likes and dislikes with your partner. When you have sex, make sure it is safe sex and that you're using protection against sexually transmitted diseases and pregnancy. Be clear with your partner about which areas of your body are okay for them to touch and which parts are off limit. Don't assume that your partner will read your mind or automatically know these things. Discussing these details may seem awkward, but it will alleviate a lot of embarrassing moments and unnecessary pain for the both of you. Relationships become stronger with open communication by helping people build trust together and minimizing the amount of unwanted surprises and hurtful feelings that can come from people making poor assumptions.

Dating violence/abuse.

Sometimes, risk doesn't show itself on the first, second, or even third date. It takes time to get to know a person, their values and personality. You may date someone for a while before learning that they're abusive or dysfunctional in relationships.

Anyone can be vulnerable to violence in a relationship, regardless of their age, gender, sexual orientation, or where they live, etc. It happens in all *types* of relationships, whether they're straight, queer or bisexual.

Violence is more than *physical harm.* Abuse can also be emotional and difficult to detect because we tend to think of violence as merely physical. People can also be emotionally abusive, manipulative and controlling. *Emotional abuse is real.* Some examples include:

- Blowing up, yelling, expressions of rage
- Being controlling and manipulative (*e.g.,* "You don't *really* love me unless you do X or Y.")
- Trying to isolate you from your friends, family, social support network
- Insulting your loved ones or peers
- Repeatedly insulting or embarrassing you in front of other people
- Wanting to know where you are at all times
- Jealousy
- Pressuring you into sex, or other decisions that aren't right for you
- Not taking responsibility for hurting you and implying all problems are *your* fault
- Refusing to respect your boundaries or needing to end the relationship; stalking you

While every relationship has its low points, like disagreements, dating abuse is recognizable because it becomes a pattern. That means that your partner continues to do and say things that are hurtful to you, even after you've told them to stop and they've apologized.

Abusive relationships often have by cycles. There are periods of extreme happiness and bliss following an argument where the hurtful partner promises to act better and does so for a while to the point where you may think the abuse is over. But the abuse happens again, followed by another apology and promises to do better. The cycle churns on and on, unless you recognize it and end the relationship. If you have a hard time breaking your emotional connection, remember these two truths:

- An abusive person cannot be reasoned with.
- You cannot change, nor is it your job, to change, dysfunctional people.

Being with an abusive person is not something that you ask for or deserve

If you're dating someone who's abusive, it's not your fault. You just got unlucky. But it can be hard to get out of the relationship sometimes, so it's not a sign of your weakness or dysfunction if you can't seem to leave. That just means you need *help.*

Experiencing dating violence as a trans person.

There are some particular factors regarding violence that you want to be aware of as a trans teen. A hurtful person will try to use your trans identity against you sometimes, as a way to convince you that you're unlovable or shameful. In an effort to manipulate and keep you in their clutches, they may say things like:

- *Do you know how lucky you are to be with me? I'm the only one who thinks you're handsome/beautiful.*
- *No one else will love you because you're trans. I'm the only one who'll love you.*
- *If you leave me, I'm going to tell everyone you're trans.*

- *Why do you hang out with those freaky trans people? You're not like them at all.*
- *I only act this way because I get a lot of crap from people for being with you.*
- *You don't need to see your family or friends. I'm the only one who really gets you.*
- *I was just kidding when I said you weren't really a girl (or boy)!*

Violence can also be physical.

- *Forcing you to engage in sexual acts or touching you in ways that feel uncomfortable or disrespectful of your gender identity.*
- *Hitting, kicking, punching, slapping, or other acts of physical aggression.*

And come in other forms as well, such as:

- *Withholding your binder, prosthetics, clothing, or puberty blockers/ hormones.*
- *Putting you in danger by outing you as trans to others.*
- *Forcing you to engage in nonconsensual sexual acts/touching.*
- *Forcing you to engage in sexual acts/touching in ways that are uncomfortable, dismissive and/or disrespectful of your gender identity.*
- *Hitting, kicking, punching, slapping, or other acts of physical aggression.*

If any of these phrases or actions sounds familiar, you should probably consider ending the relationship. While your partner may have lovable aspects and it feels good to get some of the things you want, always remember that *an abusive relationship is not going to fulfill everything you need to be the happy, healthy, whole person you're becoming.*

Reaching out for help.

Trust your gut. *Does something feel off? Are you always anxious around your date? Do you feel worse about yourself when you're around them, even if you can't put your finger on why?* If so, then it's time to move on.

Easier said than done, right? This may be the case especially, if your partner has been successful in isolating you from family and friends. You might feel like you don't have anyone to turn to. That's not the case: **There is always someone who can help**.

If you've hurt or ignored friends or loved ones because of this relationship, reach out to them, apologize, and admit that you made a mistake because you've been in a dangerous situation. Let them know you need help. It's likely they'll be happy to reconnect with you again and offer help, especially once they know why you've been absent from their lives.

If reaching out to friends doesn't work, try talking to a teacher, guidance counselor, coach, or local youth worker with whom you're comfortable. Perhaps your parents will understand and offer some advice. It can be nerve-wracking to tell others what's been happening, but once you get through it the first time, it's easier to talk about to others and you'll likely feel better too. Remember, voicing your worries and fears—whether to yourself or to others—is an incredible release for pent up emotions that you've been carrying, and the first step to making your situation better.

Many people fear when they open up about an abusive relationship, other people will say, *"Why didn't you leave sooner?" "What's wrong with you?"* Remember this: **There is nothing wrong with you**. Every relationship is a unique situation and people work through difficulties at a pace that's comfortable for them. The most important thing is your safety, and when you're feeling unsafe, then it's time to bounce.

Part of the pattern of violence is that your partner lures you back in with promises of better behavior or puts you down so much that you're truly convinced that you're not worthy of better treatment. It can be scary and easy to fall for this, especially if you have low self-esteem, which is why I began this chapter urging you to develop a healthy self-esteem before you start dating. Always remember: Never give up the things that strengthen your self-concept like your friends, family, school, and hobbies.

If you find yourself in an abusive relationship and don't know what to do and are afraid to reach out to others, you can always call an anonymous hotline.

CHAPTER 6

Social Transition

Gender transition takes a while to complete. I know that's probably hard to hear, but it's simply a fact. You can't rush through the process. Think of it as a marathon rather than a sprint and that will keep you focused and mentally balanced through your journey.

It'll take a while for you to feel settled in your body, for it to feel so familiar that you forget how uncomfortable you were before transitioning. That day will come and taking your time getting there isn't a bad thing. Everyone needs time to grow to become the person, the "whole picture," of who they are. Even though transition may feel like the most important thing in your life right now, remember to work on developing other aspects of your personality, prioritize your education, and enjoy your family and friendships along the way.

Thinking through gender expectations.

As you know, gender transitioning is about more than simply changing your body, your voice, and other visible markers of gender. The way we look, our body language, and the names and pronouns other people use in referring to us are all part of "living out" our maleness or femaleness. This is what goes into a *social transition*—which occurs before and alongside medical and legal transitioning.

Before you transition with hormones and surgery, you should think deeply about how much our ideas about gender are influenced by society. When you're transitioning, you get the chance to think about which behaviors and values feel right and natural *for you* and which ones feel wrong and uncomfortable because they are someone else's opinion of how you should act or feel. Think about the ideas society has fed you about being a man or woman and compare it to what feels right. You will likely see some differences between

your own and other people's notions. Just remember: At the end of the day, your definition of your gender is the only one that really matters.

Everyone learns subtle social "rules" about how men and women "should" look and behave. You can probably name some that are so common they've become stereotypes: Men are aggressive and women are soft; boys like blue and girls like pink; men like sports and women like more creative pursuits; and so on. The truth is that none of these things *make* someone a man or a woman. The only thing you need, to be a man or a woman, is to *know* that you are. It's as simple as that.

Still, feeling *masculine* or *feminine* is a big part of feeling like you—which means it's a big part of feeling *good* about yourself. There are many trans women who enjoy "traditional" feminine pursuits such as nurturing their family and friends, exploring clothing and makeup, spending time surrounded by other women, and pursuing other various female-oriented hobbies like cooking, gardening, and dancing.

Conversely, there are plenty of trans women who enjoy "masculine" pursuits. Being a trans woman does not mean you have to be ultra-feminine if that's not who you are. But, if that is who you are, own it and enjoy it!

There are many trans men who are more "traditionally" masculine men who enjoy competitive sports, building things, spending time surrounded by other men, and pursuing so-called "manly" hobbies like bodybuilding, fixing cars, and playing videogames.

But it would be silly to think that *all* trans men are like this or that you *have* to like masculine things in order to be a *real* man. There are plenty of trans men who have "feminine" interests, as well, which is awesome!

When you think about it, what makes dancing more lady-like and "working with your hands" more manly? Those ideas come from our society's history of men being the "providers" and women being the "homemakers." However, society evolves, too, and these roles have been changing as we learn more about gender.

Think about it. What activities make you feel proud and happy? Are they "masculine" or "feminine?" Do you feel like you *should* or *shouldn't* do them because it will make you seem more or less like a man or woman to other people?

The ultimate goal of transition is not to fit into yet another gendered box. Rather, you transition because you want to be more authentically *you*. Keep in mind that transitioning is an opportunity for you to escape boxes that have been imposed on you and the feeling of being a square peg in a round hole.

Language, clothes, and behavior.

Let's look at the shifts in words, body language, clothing, expression, and actions that affirm your gender. Seeing yourself, as well as being seen by others, as a member of your chosen gender eases a lot of emotional stress for many trans people. It can help us feel at peace.

You can begin a social transition to female or male long before hormones or surgery plays a role. This simply means living as a boy or girl without the aid of hormones or surgery.

Some of the first steps many trans teens take is changing their wardrobe, hair, voice, and tucking or binding some body parts while enhancing others with prosthetics.

Another step in social transitioning is asking others to use male or female pronouns and a new name. Telling someone that you're trans is different than seeing it. It is a new reality for them that may take some time to adjust. Remember to be patient with this process since most people have a difficult time switching pronouns and names overnight. Be kind and understanding, but don't be afraid to correct people when they use the wrong name or pronouns if they don't catch themselves first. It helps them break the old patterns of interacting with you and start a new, correct one.

Perhaps you've done some of this work already. The process isn't a one-size-fits-all model, but depends rather on how comfortable you feel in your daily environment.

For trans masculine people social transition can (but doesn't have) to include the following changes:

- Using a male-sounding or gender-neutral name
- Identifying with *"he," "him,"* and *"his"* pronouns or gender-neutral pronouns
- Wearing traditional male clothing
- Cutting one's hair short
- Foregoing jewelry and makeup
- Speaking in a lower pitch
- Using less hand or body movements when talking
- Walking with less sway in the hips and taking longer strides when walking
- Strapping down or binding the chest

- Putting a sock or penile prosthetic in the underwear (e.g., "packing")

For trans feminine people, social transition can (but doesn't have to) include:

- Using a female-sounding or gender-neutral name
- Identifying with *"she," "her,"* and *"hers"* pronouns or gender-neutral pronouns
- Wearing traditionally female clothing
- Growing one's hair longer
- Shaving the face and/or body
- Wearing jewelry and makeup
- Using more hand or body gestures when talking
- Speaking in a higher pitched voice or questioning manner
- Walking with more sway in the hips
- Strapping down the genitalia (e.g., "tucking")
- Putting socks or breast prosthetics in the bra (e.g., "padding")

All of these aspects of gender expression are visible (and audible) cues that help others read your gender. Only choose elements that help **you** feel more affirmed in your preferred gender identity. While *you* are the most important person in deciding your gender, most trans people find it vital to have others also perceive them as their true gender. Again: *Don't change yourself to become someone you're not just to fit into someone else's box.*

Of course, some things on the lists (above) are easier to change or acquire than others. While you're the only one who can control the pitch of your voice, or whether you wear a prosthetic or choose to be more expressive (or restrictive) in your gestures when talking or walking, there are other things that you may not be able to do without the aid of your parents, such as cutting (or growing out) your hair or buying and wearing the kinds of clothes you want.

You parents may be understanding of your gender transition and help you buy new clothing that's more comfortable and expresses your gender identity. If they're not helpful however, you may have friends who will help you choose clothes or teach you how to apply make-up. While I recommend having your parents be involved in as much of your social transition as possible, if you find they are unaccepting, this doesn't mean that your situation is hopeless or that you will never be able to transition. You will be your own adult someday and will get the chance to make decisions for yourself. So, try to maintain a respectful relationship with your parents until then.

Social transitioning for trans men.

People who are assigned "female" at birth have a unique set of considerations when they want to be seen as "male" (likewise for trans women, which I'll address later in this section). Some of these goals are achievable without hormones or surgery, while others, like growing taller or having bigger feet or hands, may not be changeable. Loving yourself means accepting this reality!

While you won't be able to grow facial hair or have a naturally flat chest without hormones and surgery, you can still do a lot to alter your physical appearance. Let's look at some steps you can take. *These are not requirements, and there is no definitive order that you must follow. Do what feels right to you.*

Picking a new name.

You can use a gender-neutral or masculine nickname. Some people choose to use a masculine version of the name that their parents gave them at birth. Examples are: Patrick (from Patricia), Loren (from Lauren), or Angel or Angelo (from Angela). The advantage of this is your new chosen name is easier for people to remember than a new name that bears no resemblance to your birth name. Sometimes people also choose to turn their birth names into initials. For example, they may turn a birth name like "Jenny Rae" into "J.R.," or "Seth Jamison" into "S.J." If you can't think of a name that you like, there are many books listing baby names that are a great place to start. There are also many places online where you can find names by simply Googling: *"male names"* or *"masculine names."*

Shopping in the men's department.

You'll probably want to replace skirts, blouses, dresses, heels, and halters for button down shirts, jeans, t-shirts, boots, and ties. You may also want to abandon makeup and lots of jewelry, if you feel that it will interfere with how others see you.

Going to the barbershop.

This is often one of the most daunting and thrilling parts of social transitioning. Barbershops are the best place to go because they specialize in men's haircuts, using tools and techniques that achieve hairlines that read as more "masculine." If you feel like you cannot go to the barbershop in your neighborhood, research others surrounding your area, bring a friend, and try to make a fun trip of it.

Lowering your voice.

At first, it can feel awkward trying to speak "deeper," but it comes naturally after a little practice. When trying to speak in a lower voice, don't try to go too low—just a couple notes below your usual speaking voice. Practice keeping your pitch down, keeping a steady tone, and try not to end sentences with question marks or in a higher pitch, because these cues can sound "feminine" to English speakers who've been trained to cue in to speech patterns along gender lines. Also, be aware that forcing your voice higher or lower can affect your vocal chords and cause nodules to develop. Like all vocalists, learn how to warm up your voice to avoid damaging your vocal chords. Get a tape recorder and practice your new speaking voice. Record yourself in the tone you were socialized to speak and compare it to the lower tones you're trying to achieve. This will give you a better sense of the differences between your "feminine" and "masculine" speech patterns and tones.

Adjusting your walk and mannerisms.

Observe the men around you and practice walking with less side-to-side hip movement if that feels comfortable. Men tend to take longer strides when they walk and sway their shoulders more than women, but be careful not to exaggerate this. When you speak, moreover, look people directly in the eyes and try to use less hand gestures.

Binding your chest.

The shape of one's chest is often the first thing others look for when trying to assess whether someone is a man or woman. It's done automatically and instantaneously—we all do it—without thinking. Many men choose to flatten their chest by strapping down their breasts, which is known as "binding." This should be something you use for relating to others, but when you're alone at night, **take your binder off the give your body a break.** You should never sleep with your binder on because it is unhealthy to squeeze your chest and stomach in something so tight for such a long period of time. While I do not recommend working out in a binder, if you do, make sure your binder allows for ample movement and doesn't cause discomfort or pain. Working out causes your muscles and fat to change shape, and a tight binder can force your body to develop in a way that will hurt you. You could break a rib or puncture a lung. Binders are meant to be temporary. Follow the guidelines from binder distributors and doctors, and don't wear them for an extended period of time.

Furthermore, if you choose to bind, **don't use ace bandages**, because this method restricts your ribcage's ability to expand and dangerously lowers your oxygen intake. Some men use duct-tape to bind their chest, but I don't recommend that either because, it can (and will) damage your skin in the long run. It's better to purchase a chest binder, if possible, from companies that specialize in trans masculine items like Underworks or FTM Kingdom, which you can find online. Another alternative to duct-tape and ace bandages is to wear an athletic bra—maybe two—covered by a couple of layers of clothing over them. *(See Appendix IV.)*

Create a bulge "down there."

This visible cue isn't as important as your chest, because it's not the first thing other people look for when determining someone's gender. That doesn't mean it's not important to you. You may feel that it's necessary to "feel" a bulge in your pants and feel a boost of confidence with a prosthetic in your underwear. If so, you can purchase a packer and there are many *options (See Appendix IV.)* If you cannot get a packer, try a rolled up sock instead. Either way, think carefully about size. You want to choose a size that's comfortable for you, *while also being subtle and not drawing too much attention to your genital region.* If you choose to use a sock, remember to secure in it your underwear with a safety pin, for it will move around and shift when you're going about your day, and you don't want it to fall out of your pants in public or shift to an "unnatural" looking position that draws unwanted stares from people. Packing also helps you get used to feeling weight in your pants if you decide someday to go forward with genital reconstruction surgery.

Social transitioning for trans women.

People who are assigned "male" at birth also have a unique set of considerations when aiming to be perceived socially as "female." Just like with trans men, some of these goals are achievable without hormones or surgery, and some, like being shorter or having smaller feet or hands may not be changeable, and loving yourself means accepting that!

While you won't be able to permanently remove facial hair without electrolysis[13] or an Adam's apple without surgery, you can do plenty to alter your physical appearance. Let's look at some possible steps that trans women might take. *These are not requirements though, and there is no definitive order that you have to follow. Do what feels right to you.*

Picking a new name.

As I suggested for trans men, you can use a gender-neutral or feminine nickname. Some people choose to use a feminine version of the name that their parents gave them. Examples are: Leandra (from Lenny or Leonard); Melanie (from Mel or Melvin); or Natalie (from Nathan or Nathaniel). The advantage of this is that your new chosen name is easier for people to remember because it resembles the name they've always called you. Sometimes people choose to turn their birth names into initials instead. If you can't think of a name that you like, there are also many books listing baby names that are a great place to start. And there are many places online also where you can find names by simply Googling: *"female names"* or *"feminine names."*

Shopping the women's department.

Choose clothing that feels comfortable to you as a woman and your own

13 Electrolysis- hair removal.

definition of womanhood. That may be blouses, dresses, skirts, heels, etc. You may want to consider wearing more makeup and jewelry.

Going to the salon.

Salons are often the best places to go because they specialize in hair styles for women. As I suggested for transmen, if you aren't comfortable going to a hairstylist in your neighborhood, find a salon elsewhere and bring a friend for support.

Changing your voice.

Although there are exceptions, women's voices tend to have a higher pitch than men's and vary in intonation. Women will often finish their sentences in a lilt or higher pitch, sometimes sounding more like a question than a direct statement. If this is appealing to you, practice your speaking voice by moving your pitch up and down and varying your tone. These speech patterns tend to sound "feminine" to English speakers. Note, unlike the effects that testosterone has on trans men, hormones for trans women do not have any effect on their voices. So, working with a vocal coach or speech therapist, can be helpful. YouTube is also an excellent place to find free coaching.

Get a tape recorder and practice your new speaking voice. Record yourself in the tone you were socialized to speak and compare it to the higher pitches you're trying to incorporate. This will give you a better sense of the differences between your "feminine" and "masculine" speech patterns and tones. You may feel awkward at first trying to change your pitch and speech patterns at first, but with practice it'll eventually feel natural.

Adjusting your walk and mannerisms.

Observe women around you and practice their walking patterns. Women tend to walk with more side-to-side sway in their hips. When you speak, consider using your hands more freely while expressing yourself.

Enhancing your curves.

The shape of one's body is often the first thing others look at when trying to assess someone's gender from afar. Many trans women choose to change their body profile to be curvier by enhancing their breasts, hips, and buttocks. This can be achieved by purchasing a padded bra or padded underwear or buying silicone inserts held down by compression undergarments. *(See Appendix IV.)*

This can be expensive, so some women use homemade methods with foam or rolled up fabrics instead. Whichever method you try, remember this: **Never inject or allow anyone else to inject silicone directly into your breasts.** This method, known as "pumping," is extremely dangerous and can easily result in injury and even death.

Tucking in "down there."

Some women feel more confident and safer when their lower parts aren't visible as a bulge. Some women wear tight underwear, sometimes several layers, to compress their genitals more closely between their legs, or use tape to hold down their genitals although that will likely cause discomfort and isn't recommended. Other women wear a special kind of underwear called a *gaff* that's designed to comfortably flatten their genitalia. Just make sure that whenever you're using compression clothing—whether it is for your genitalia or for padding—that you give your body a break by taking it off at night while you sleep. There are videos on YouTube that show to create your own gaff.

All of these steps are things you can do to transition effectively without hormones and surgery and help you to feel affirmed in your gender while also signaling it to others. Taking some of these measures may help you feel like you're working towards accomplishing your goals, when you're feeling frustrated that things aren't moving fast enough.

A Note on "passing."[14]

When you listen to transgender and cis-gender (non-trans) people talk about transitioning, you may hear the word *"passing"* being thrown around. This term refers to a trans person being read as their preferred gender. This is a goal, depending upon the environment, for a lot of trans people, but it's also okay if you don't feel the need to *"pass."*

Many trans people pass for safety depending on their situation. For instance, if you are around strangers or in a public sex-segregated area (like a bathroom or locker room), *passing can be a means of survival and moving through a space without being harassed.*

Some trans people pass because they just want to feel included in their gender group—like "one of the guys" or "one of the girls"—which can be a tremendous relief. It's perfectly acceptable to want others to see you as the gender you know yourself to be.

However, sometimes the pressure to pass can generate feelings of shame. Some people may tell you you're being "dishonest" and should be rejected for trying to

14 I am not fond of this term. However, for explanation purposes I will use the term "passing" to educate you about the concept. I prefer the terminology, "recognized as the person you know yourself to be" because it's more positive.

"hide" or "trick" people. Or they may say that you're not a real woman or man if they can "tell" you were assigned a different gender at birth.

Don't believe them!

There's no appropriate, or right way to be trans. Many trans people identify somewhere in between male and female, masculine and feminine. Maybe you are a trans guy who likes having long hair. Maybe you are a trans woman who enjoys working with power tools and outdoor activities. That is perfectly fine. How you express yourself is *your* choice.

Remember: You do you!

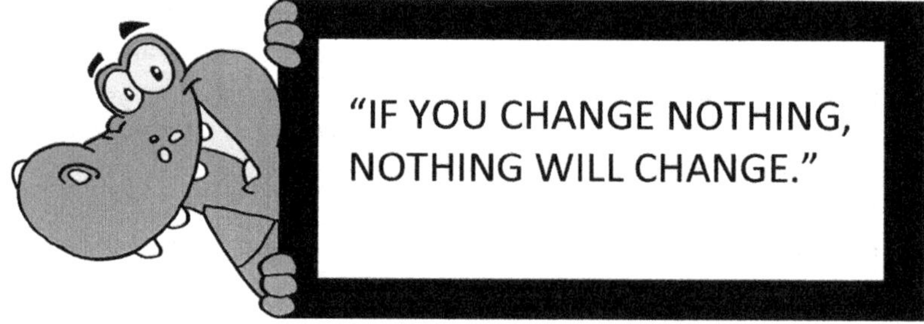

CHAPTER 7

Medical

Before I get into a discussion of hormones, you should know that many people transition socially and don't want to take hormones or change their physical body. This decision is an individual one that only you can decide.

Finding a doctor.

Some "regular" doctors such as primary care physicians and general family practitioners can oversee your medical transition. It's even better if you can find a *pediatric endocrinologist*—a doctor who specializes in hormones for children and youth. Some primary care physicians may be willing, to work with a pediatric endocrinologist to oversee your hormonal transition.

If your parents are on board with your medical transition, you may want to ask them to accompany you to your family practitioner to discuss your options of hormonal transitioning. Keep in mind though, that some doctors require you to get a letter of evaluation from a licensed therapist who says you can begin hormones.

It is essential that you work with a doctor when using any kind of puberty blockers and/or hormones, rather than obtaining them from a friend, the Internet, or the street.

Why? Because doctors monitor your body's hormone levels by taking blood samples and they know which signs to look for if you're dosage is too high or too low. Too much of certain hormones in your body can adversely affect your bone health, liver, heart and more. For trans masculine and male identified people, there's the risk of accumulating too much testosterone in your body,

which will then convert to estrogen and produce unwanted feminizing effects in your body. In addition, if you obtain hormones from a nonmedical source, you can never be certain what you're really putting in your body. Trans people have been tricked by con artists posing as "medical experts" whose sole goal was to exploit and make money from their urgent need to transition. This also applies for purchasing hormones on the Internet.

If you use a needle and syringe to inject your hormones, do not borrow someone else's instruments to inject yourself. Why? Because you can never be certain that their instruments are clean and free of disease. You can contract diseases like Hepatitis C and HIV if you use the needle and syringe of someone who is infected. There have been a few cases where trans men have contracted HIV from using the needle of an HIV+ person to inject testosterone into their bodies. If you require needles and syringes to administer your hormones, it is best to purchase them from the pharmacy or go to a hospital to get them.

Puberty blockers.

Even before signs of puberty emerge, hormones begin making unseen changes inside your body. If you are going to an endocrinologist prior to puberty, they will check the hormones in your blood levels to monitor when they start changing, which may begin around the age of nine or ten. Without the blood work though, you wouldn't be able to tell the external physical effects of hormones until you're around 11 years-old or puberty.

The "sex" hormones (estrogen/progesterone for cis-females and testosterone for cis-males), actually regulate a lot of functions in our bodies. But they are most notable as chemical messengers that tell our bodies to produce certain secondary sex characteristics like facial hair growth for men and breast growth for women. These processes can be suppressed with *puberty blockers* if they are administered early enough, preferably *before* the onset of puberty.

Trans women with access to puberty blockers use them sometimes to *delay or prevent* facial hair, an Adam's apple, and a lower voice from developing, while trans men use them to keep from developing breasts and hips and starting menstruation. People do this sometimes so they can have more time to decide whether they want to take hormones later and how they want their bodies to develop.

While puberty blockers prevent the hormones that trigger changes in your body that you don't want, cross-hormone, or hormone replacement therapy (HRT) triggers the changes you do want. After being on puberty suppressants for a few years, some trans people choose to go on the hormone that will further masculinize (testosterone) or feminize (estrogen/and possibly progesterone) their bodies. If a person goes straight from using puberty blockers into cross-hormone therapy, they won't have to contend with the secondary sex characteristics of their birth sex in the same way as someone who did not take hormone blockers and allowed puberty to change their body. For instance, if a trans boy starts hormone blockers before puberty and follows that up with testosterone, the chances of him growing breasts are slim to none. Likewise, a trans girl's voice will likely not deepen, nor will she grow an Adam's apple or a beard if she starts puberty blockers early enough and then switches to estrogen. Some young trans women following this course could experience a little breast development.

To begin puberty blocking and HRT, you'll need to get permission from your parents, as most doctors require formal parental consent to treat you. **I do not advise you to seek treatment from anyone other than a board certified physician.** If you can't get parental permission you may have to wait a little while before beginning HRT until you reach the legal age. Go back and check out Chapter 6 on Social Transition to remind yourself of steps you can take to feel like you're expressing your true self, regardless of whether you're on blockers or hormones. Know that you're not alone in this experience. There are many other young trans people experiencing the same thing and you can find them online and in books. *(See Appendix VII.)*

Hormone replacement therapy.

Cis-males and cis-females have both estrogen and testosterone in their system. Estrogen helps with bone growth and testosterone helps in building muscle and sex drive. These hormones affect the secondary sex characteristics.

HRT changes the balance of these powerful chemical messengers. For teens transitioning from male to female, testosterone is generally suppressed with spironolactone (*spiro*-antiandrogen)[15] therefore allowing a lower and healthier amount of estrogen to be taken. For trans boys, simply adding testosterone will overpower the effects of estrogen and progesterone in the body. **Remember: Never take more than your doctor prescribes!**

What to expect in general from HRT.

Before starting HRT, it's important to understand what hormones do and *don't* do, so you have realistic expectations of how your body may change. The rule of hormones: they can give to the body, but they cannot take away. This is why many trans people also have surgery to further change their body to match their gender.

15 Anti-androgen: medicine given to counteract testosterone in transwomen.

Hormones work on the soft tissues of your body but do not alter your skeleton.

Testosterone or estrogen affects the body's skin, fat, and muscles, but cannot alter the underlying skeletal structure. This means that hormones, for the most part, cannot make you taller or shorter, or make your hands and shoulders smaller or larger. This is especially the case when puberty hasn't been suppressed and the body has undergone secondary sex characteristic development. For example, estrogen will not reduce a trans girl's or woman's Adam's apple or change her voice to a higher pitch, if she has already gone through puberty, but it will lower a trans man's voice whether he's undergone puberty or not.

Certain changes are permanent.

You might think: *Sure, that's the point*. And, it is for many trans people, but it's still important to know what changes are permanent and can't be altered. Hormones work at different rates on different bodies, so their effects may take more or less time to appear for you, but you can expect that once you "grow" anything with hormones, it's there to stay. For example: for trans women, this includes breasts and for trans men it includes facial hair, lower voice, and male pattern baldness. I'll talk more about the specific effects of each hormone later in this chapter.

Certain effects are only retained while you remain on HRT.

If you stop taking hormones, certain effects, like the amount of hair (or change in the hair line), presence (or absence) of acne, emotions, ability to gain or lose muscle, and your redistribution of fat (e.g., more or less "padding" on your hips, stomach, and face,) will gradually shift back to where you were before beginning HRT. Trans people have many reasons for stopping HRT. Sometimes people quit for health reasons or it's too expensive. Others stop because they want to have children, or they identify as gender ambiguous or gender queer and are aiming for a "middle ground" in their gender expression. Whatever your reasons, just remember that some physical changes may not be reversible, and it's best to consult the doctor who's prescribing them for you about the impact of going off HRT.

More hormones do not equal a faster transition.

The second rule of hormones: Only take the dosage that your doctor prescribes for you. Your doctor will regularly require blood tests to find out if your hormone levels are in a zone that's appropriate for a woman or man your age. You should never take more hormones than what your physician says, because an excess of estrogen can cause blood clots, migraines, and autoimmune disorders (diseases where your immune system attacks your body). Likewise, an excess of testosterone can hurt your liver, raise your cholesterol, and thicken your blood. An additional warning to trans masculine and male identified people: If you take more testosterone than your body needs, your body can (and will likely) convert it into estrogen, which will feminize your body in ways that you're trying to escape. So taking more hormones won't get you to your goal faster, and it could be counterproductive, not to mention causing permanent damage. As far as hormones are concerned, slow is better. Remember: Transitioning is a marathon—not a 100 yard dash!

Certain surgeries require hormone use beforehand.

Since hormones inspire physical changes in certain body parts, you will need to wait for their effects to take hold before you can complete certain surgeries. For trans feminine or female identified people, this means waiting for your breasts to grow if you want breast augmentation, and waiting for your face to reshape itself before getting facial feminization surgery. For trans men, it means waiting for your genitals (clitoris) to grow a bit, if you want genital reconstruction.

Hormones aren't as important for some surgeries such as chest reconstruction for trans men. Incidentally, puberty blockers can be helpful in some surgeries for trans masculine and male youth because they suppress breast development and lessen the amount of tissue needing to be removed and reshaped. Similarly, shaving the trachea to reduce the Adam's apple, and electrolysis to remove unwanted hair, can occur at any time. Puberty blockers prescribed for trans feminine and female youth can also suppress the masculinization of their facial features and tracheal growth.

Hormones work best when you're taking care of your body.

Now, you have another powerful reason to avoid smoking, drinking, or doing drugs. Seriously! Your body is growing new tissue and changing the tissue that's already apparent. You can help your hormonal transition by staying as healthy as possible. Just like a good parent who is gentle and caring with a growing child, you need to treat your body the same way. Get enough sleep and exercise, watch your nutrition and what you eat. Avoid cigarettes, drugs, soda, and processed foods and figure out ways to reduce stress in your life by laughing, relaxing, meditating, playing video games, or pursuing a new activities or outlets.

It can take a few months before you begin to see changes with HRT. Ultimately, it's a wait-and-see game. That's because hormones work gradually on the body—everyone's body, including cis-gender people—so you can't expect them to work any faster on you. This can be a difficult period in your transition because you've been waiting forever to be your true self and have others see you as such. You may even feel like everyone else around you has their gender down pat while you're still trying to sprout breasts or facial or chest hair. That's simply how hormones work. So hunker down and prepare yourself mentally for the long haul, be patient, and learn to celebrate the small advances your body is making daily. Chart the changes that happen to you because it's hard to see them on a daily basis. But you can take videos and pictures and compare them to see how much progress you're making. You'll be amazed at how much you have actually changed in a few months' time. *(See Appendix IX.)*

HRT for trans women.

Every trans girl or woman responds differently to hormone therapy. Some women see changes in their bodies very quickly while others wait months or even a year or two before noticing changes. Some changes, like a shift in emotions, are less obvious than others that may be more visible such as breast growth. Just remember that taking more estrogen than what your doctor prescribes will not speed up the changes, and could cause health complications. So be patient!

Trans women who combine estrogen with spironolactone (spiro) are able to raise the levels of estrogen in their body because spiro suppresses testosterone. When deciding between delivery methods of estrogen, women usually consider factors (which your parents will likely be considering if they're involved in your healthcare): 1) your comfort, 2) the cost, 3) efficiency. Your doctor, if knowledgeable should be able to guide you.

The most common and affordable form of administering hormone therapy is oral, usually taking pills. However, this may increase your likelihood for blood clots. So women use an estrogen patch, cream, or a spray as an alternative method. Many women inject estrogen because some feel it's a more efficient method. However, this method can result in the fluctuation of your hormone levels that may lead to mood swings, hot flashes, migraines, anxiety, or weight gain.

Lastly, many, though not all, women take progesterone[16] for the added benefits of improving their energy and stabilizing their moods, getting more breast development and/or redistributing their body fat.

Effects of transfeminine HRT.[17]

Your body will gradually show the effects of hormones after you begin using them, often starting within a few weeks. No two women exhibit exactly the same effects, and they never occur at exactly the same rate.

This is a really exciting time. So enjoy the process! You can expect some of these changes sooner or later in varying degrees:

- Skin becomes thinner, drier, and less oily and softer
- Decrease in sweat and body odor
- Fat shifts away from the legs to the hips and thighs
- Fat shifts in the face, making it rounder (less angular) or softer
- Decrease in ability to gain and maintain muscle mass

16 Providers and patients debate the benefits of progestogens.

17 See *Appendix X.*

- Increase in touch sensitivity, especially in the fingers
- Increase in smell and/or taste sensitivity
- Genital (especially testicular) shrinkage
- Decline in spontaneous erections
- Thinning of hair on the face, chest, and possible everywhere, but will not remove the beard
- Increase in ability to cry and/or feelings of calmness
- Sterility (inability to impregnate) within several months
- Increase in confidence from feeling more at ease with one's body

Important note:

1. While undergoing HRT, some trans women still get electrolysis to remove unwanted hair on their face and body, and
2. Hormones do not change the depth of the voice or receding/balding hair. Neither will it reduce the trachea or Adam's apple if it's already developed.

HRT for trans men.

Every man has a different response to testosterone. Some men see changes in their body very quickly, and others will wait months or even a couple years. Taking more "T" (as "testosterone" is often called) will not speed up the effects, and may actually cause health complications (as I previously explained regarding estrogen for trans women)—so be patient!

Testosterone is most commonly injected, but some men also use gels, creams, or pellets, which are placed under the skin. Before you start using testosterone, the doctor will check the hormone levels in your blood and determine the dose that's right for your body and age. They'll regularly check your blood every few months to see that your T-level is within the healthy range for men of your age.

When deciding between injections, gels/creams (like Androgel or Testim)—or pellets, (Testopel), men usually consider a few factors (which your parents will be considering if they're involved in your healthcare): 1) comfort, 2) cost 3) efficiency.

Many men don't like needles, much less, a subcutaneous injection (SubQ), which is under the skin. The idea of injecting your thigh or buttocks with an intramuscular "(IM)" can feel daunting and scary. Injections are usually administered every week or two weeks, depending on what you decide with your doctor.

Some trans men enlist family members, friends, or significant others to help with their injections or to provide moral support while they do it themselves.

Don't try to inject yourself the first time. Get a nurse, doctor or some other healthcare professional to inject you first and teach you the proper procedure before doing it yourself. Ask questions when they're showing you the procedure. Don't just follow YouTube videos on the Internet. While vlogs of other trans men injecting can be helpful, it's best to rely on a trained professional to show you how to inject.

Some men prefer a testosterone cream or gel to avoid the needle altogether, and/or if they want the changes to occur slower. It can be more comfortable to rub a gel into your shoulder area than injecting a needle in your thigh or buttocks. The only catch is that gels and creams tend to be more expensive than injectable "T" and you have to remember to do it every day. There are some men who worry about transferring the gel to children or female-identified loved ones who do not want to experience the effects of testosterone. To avoid this unwanted transference, make sure you rub the gel or cream in fully and then cover that area before touching anyone else. Then wash your hands thoroughly.

Effects of transmasculine HRT.[18]

Your body will gradually show the effects of T after you start using it. The effects will be slower with a T gel or cream. No two men exhibit exactly the same effects, and they never occur at the exact same rate.

Watching your body change is an exciting time. Some of the changes you may experience are:

- Thicker, more oily skin (and some men develop acne)
- A "musky" change in body odor
- Fat shifts away from the hips to the stomach
- Fat shifts in the face and facial muscles thicken to give a more angular shape
- Ability to gain and maintain muscle mass
- Increase in appetite
- Decline in touch sensitivity, including temperature gauge in the fingertips (*not all men experience this*)
- Clitoral/penile growth (*~1-5 cm*)
- Deepening voice
- Increase in hair growth on the face, chest, and possibly all over
- Receding hairline, balding and "male pattern" baldness
- Shift in emotional range; a decrease in the ability to cry

18 See *Appendix X.*

- Feelings of assertiveness, and for some, feelings of aggression (some men also experience emotional calmness)
- Increase in sex drive
- Cessation of the period/decline in ability to conceive
- Increased confidence from feeling more at ease with one's body

Most of these changes will come in time as you undergo hormone therapy. Don't be discouraged if you don't immediately see changes. Remember that changes *are happening* inside of you even if you can't see them.

One thing that you can do to help is keep track of your body changes. There are many ways to do this. You can start off by measuring your chest, waist, calves, biceps, etc. I went nuts when I first started T and kept a log of measurements of my wrists, head, feet, even the space between the top of my nose to my hairline. I kept a careful log of any change that could be measured. Write the numbers down and do the measurements again every three months. You're bound to see the small changes that way.[19]

You can also take pictures when you start HRT and chronicle your changes by recording videos of yourself. Many trans people post vlogs of their hormonal transition on YouTube for example. Some people talk about the changes every week or every month. It is up to you how you want to do it. Not only are you capturing the way you look and sound, but you may also want to talk about other things that are changing around you as well.

Pictures, videos, and measurements can come in handy sometimes when you're feeling like your body isn't changing as fast as you'd like. When you look back on where you started, or simply where you were three months ago, you'll be able to see the changes which have been so hard to see on a daily basis.

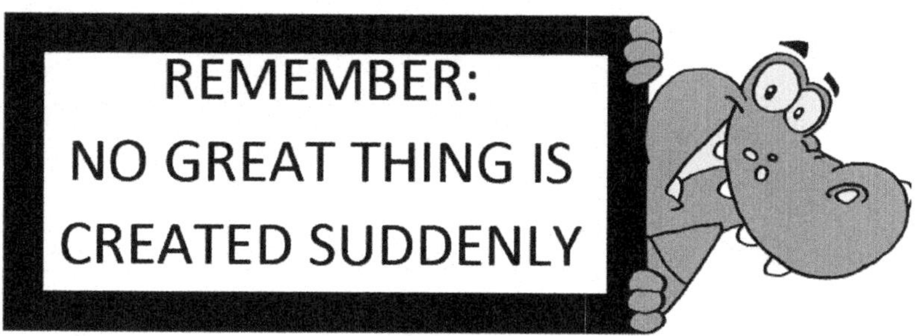

19 See *Appendix IX.*

CHAPTER 8

Gender Surgeries[20]

You may be thinking about gender reassignment (or affirmation) surgery. Decisions about surgery should never be taken lightly or hurried. There are many questions you need to ask yourself, and a lot of information you need to gather before making decisions. That's because most surgeries are expensive, complicated, often painful and largely irreversible. Once you have them, especially genital reconstruction, they cannot be undone. They are also rarely covered by medical insurance. [21]

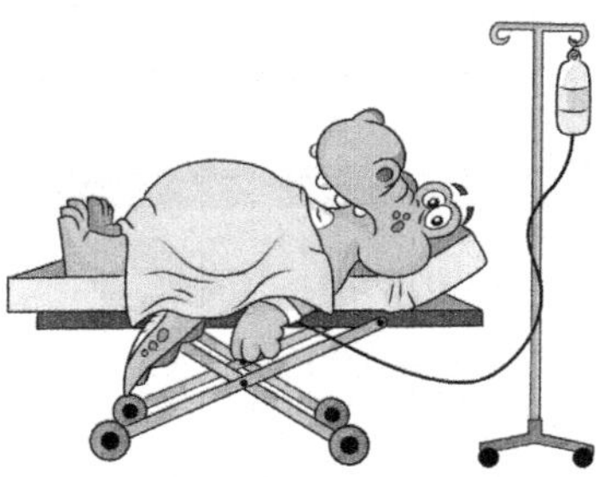

There are many kinds of gender affirming surgeries, and the messages we receive from mainstream media about them are often false and misinforming. You must do careful research when making decisions about surgery, including whether surgery is right for you and if so, whether you need it right now, or can wait until later. How important is it to you? How will surgery make your life better? If you can't afford or get permission to have surgery right now, what are you going to do in the meantime to take care of yourself? What can you do proactively to work towards your surgical goal? What kind surgery is best for you and who should do it? You don't have to decide right now. You have plenty of time to think about these questions.

As a teen, decision making around surgery may be largely out of your hands because of money, age or both. If you're under the age of 18, you'll need to obtain your parents' permission for surgery. If your family can't afford or is unwilling to pay for your surgery, remember that, it's only a temporary setback. Most of these

20 General surgical information is taken from *Trans Bodies, Trans Selves,* edited by Laura Erickson-Schroth.

21 This is beginning to change in many states.

surgeries can be done once you are old enough. If you have been on puberty-blockers, you may be able to avoid some surgeries.

So, if you can't get surgery now that shouldn't stop you from researching and making plans for your future. Start planning now, so that when you are able to have surgery, you'll be ready. If you have a job, you can start putting money away in a savings account to use for surgery later. You can begin following a good nutritional and exercise program that targets your body mass index (BMI) and cardiovascular system to prepare your body. The better your health is, the stronger your chances are for a faster recovery and better surgical results. *(Appendix VI for more information.)*

Finding a surgeon.

When the time comes, you'll want to think carefully about who's going to be reconstructing your body. You can do a search online for plastic surgeons and start checking out their websites. Many surgeons work with both men and women while some surgeons only work with women and others only work with men.

There are several surgical techniques that surgeons use to reconstruct your face, chest, or genitals, so start looking at pictures of the surgeon's results if they are accessible online. You can also do a general search for the surgeon's name to try to find pictures that patients have posted elsewhere online. In *Appendix VI* you can find resources for locating surgeons.

It's important that surgeons and their staff treat you with respect—sometimes referred to as "good bedside manner"—and that you feel safe and taken care of. When picking a surgeon, search online for reviews from their past trans clients because their experience can give you a sense of how the doctor views and handles trans patients. Call or email the surgeon and ask questions. Write a list of questions beforehand and make sure the surgeon answers all of them. Take note of how they respond. Do they take time to fully answer your questions? Ask if you can talk to previous patients they've operated on and be suspicious if a surgeon says no patients are available to speak with. Ask the surgeon's patients if they are happy with their surgical results.

Once you decide on a surgeon, you can begin thinking about costs and how you're going to pay for it. Remember to factor in the anesthesiologist's fee and hospitalization costs (if a stay is necessary). You may also have to travel, which might mean additional costs for hotel, food, transportation to and from the doctor's office, and for follow-up appointments.

Electrolysis.

Trans men and trans women may need electrolysis, whether it is for hair removal on the face or to prepare for surgery. It can be one of the most difficult procedures of surgical transitioning. (If you are on puberty blockers as a trans woman you may not need to have electrolysis on your face because hair will not grow.) However, if you do have hair, there is a possibility that being on estrogen may slow the growth or thin your facial hair. Every face is different! Trans men will grow hair from testosterone and may have to remove it from their arm, leg or another area for bottom surgery.

It is not wise to use a hair removal cream (depilatory) on your face. It doesn't really work for trans women, because it's designed for ciswomen who have "peach fuzz" and doesn't affect the hair root. Electrolysis, on the other hand, is very successful at killing the roots, but if you have a lot of hair (beard), it is a long painful process that may require pain medicine or a topical anesthetic on your face.

Laser hair reduction is also a possibility. The beam can cover a larger area, but the laser is only good for removal of dark hair. People with dark skin or light facial hair are not good candidates. Some of the side effects of both electrolysis and laser hair removal are:

- Redness or swelling of the treated area
- Mild bleeding or scabs

Gender-affirming surgeries for trans men.
Top surgery.

There are number of options of top surgery, (chest reconstruction), for trans men that are based upon their chest size and shape. Your surgeon will be able to determine which technique is best for you depending on your chest contour. The majority of men get a ***double incision with nipple/areola grafting,*** (also known as a *double mastectomy, or double incision; DI.)* This involves cutting an opening below each breast, removing the nipples and paring them down to a smaller size, taking out excess breast tissue, and then sewing up the chest and reattaching the nipples in a higher location that's more typical of male torsos. Usually after the DI procedure, there are two medical drains to collect excess blood and lymphatic fluid for a few days or a week. Most doctors require patients wear a compression vest for a certain amount of time after surgery, usually one or two weeks. Every doctor has their own procedure. That is why you need to do your own research and educate yourself.

Some down sides to this surgery are:

- Scarring

- Potential nipple graft loss
- Partial/complete loss of nipple sensation
- Nipple size and placement may uneven or asymmetrical
- Dogs ears under arms (which can be corrected with surgical revision)
- Possible puckering along the scars
- Permanent numbness in different areas
- Risks of *any* surgery: infection, bleeding, complications from anesthesia, blood clots and death (which is extremely rare)

Another surgery that's currently gaining more ground is the *Inverted-T/T-Anchor.* Originally, this surgery was used for breast reduction, but has now emerged as a popular surgery for medium to large chested men because the nipple-areola complex can be retained for good sensation. There is a scar under each breast and a vertical cut upward to the nipple. The nipple is removed in its entirety with no nerves or blood supply severed. The breast tissue is then removed and the nipples replaced in a position that's more typical for male bodies. (Many of the downsides above apply to this surgery).

The third kind of top surgery is called the *peri-areolar procedure.* It involves cutting small holes around the nipple to remove excess tissue and replacing the nipple. This procedure is usually for men with very small breasts with and A cup size or less.

The last surgery is subcutaneous mastectomy (sometimes called a *"keyhole procedure"*) and is slightly different because the surgeon only makes a small incision half-way around the bottom of the nipple. Liposuction is used to remove the breast tissue from under the skin and the nipple is sometimes resized. Nipple-areola sensation is usually maintained in this surgery.

While the double incision or anchor leaves most men with scars, its benefit is that it can be performed on men of all sizes—though a doctor may caution some clients to lose weight beforehand so that the best results can be achieved. If not, extra skin can gather under the armpits and leave a pointed (dog ear) look below the armpit. The *keyhole/peri-areolar* benefit is that it leaves sensation and minimal scarring, but only a fraction of men are eligible for it, and not every surgeon is experienced in it, so do your research! However, here's something to remember; If you are fortunate enough to go on puberty-blockers at the right time, you may not need top surgery at all. Ultimately though, you need to talk with a doctor to get the best advice about the various ways that hormones interact with and impact surgery.

Beyond chest reconstruction, some men choose to have ***liposuction*** (removal of fat), to shape their chest and torsos. A few men with small chests opt to have liposuction on their breasts instead of surgery. Other men opt for liposuction on the stomach and waist to achieve the more typical "straight waist" of an average male versus the "curvier" hips that some trans men have.

Bottom surgery.

Genital reconstructions—also known as "bottom surgery"—are divided into two categories. A minimally invasive procedure is the ***metoidioplasty***, which cuts ligaments surrounding a clitoris/phallus (usually enhanced in size by testosterone) to allow it to protrude further from the body. Some men pair this with a ***scrotoplasty***, which is the creation of testicles from the skin of the labia combined with scrotal implants or fat, and/or an ***urethraplasty***, which allows you to urinate from your penis while standing up.

Men can also opt for a ***phalloplasty***, which is the creation of a penis from tissue grafts taken from another part of the body. If a man has a *metoidioplasty*, he can still have phalloplasty later. Certain types of phalloplasty may require you to have electrolysis to remove hair follicles almost a year in advance.

To create a phallus in this procedure, tissue is taken from either:

- The forearm (RFF–Radial Forearm Flap),
- The side of the chest (MLD–Musculocutaneous Latissimus Dorsi)
- Abdomen, (Abdominal Phalloplasty–Conjoined Bilateral Pedicle Groin Flap, Gilles/Suitcase handle)
- Thigh (ALT–Anterolateral Thigh Flap)

There are more types of surgeries. The ones named above are the most performed.[22]

Phalloplasty typically results in unavoidable scarring at the skin donor site where the tissue is taken to form the penis. At the same time however, phalloplasty tends to result in a larger, more traditional looking penis. Inserts or pumps can be implanted in your penis so that you can have an erection. Phalloplasty can also pair with other genital reconstruction procedures like scrotoplasty and urethraplasty, mons-resection (removal of pubic fat), liposuction, vaginectomy or colpoclesis (closing of the vagina) and total hysterectomy (removal of the uterus, cervix and ovaries.)

Certain risks come with these surgeries as well:

- Phalloplasty can require multiple surgical stages and revisions.
- Procedures can be painful and require time to recover.
- Could have visible scarring.

22 This is a great website for beginning of FTM transitions: http://www.ftmguide.org/

- Skin grafting could have skin death (necrosis) and loss of some or all of penis.
- Implants in testicles can extrude and force their way out and require removal and subsequent surgery to re-implant.
- The narrowing, blockage or leakage of the new urethra.
- Nerve damage at the donor site (the place where skin was taken from) could occur.
- Erotic sensation could be changed or diminished.
- Result may not be aesthetically pleasing.
- Infections, hematomas (collection of blood) and other postoperative problems can occur.

Some guys get partial genital reconstruction (metoidioplasty or phalloplasty without other surgeries) because they like their vaginas and want to keep them intact. There are some surgeons who will let you do this. A vaginectomy is no longer considered necessary for scrotoplasty, urethtraplasty, or phalloplasty by some doctors. Remember, if you have a hysterectomy you will no longer be able to menstruate or give birth, and if you have an oophorectomy, you will not be able to use your own eggs to reproduce. Some trans guys are having some of their eggs frozen before having an oophorectomy in the hope of using them for *in vitro* fertilization at a later time.

I know that this is a lot of information to digest at one time and you may be feeling a bit overwhelmed. The most important thing to remember when doing your research is that you are in control of the surgical procedures that you are willing to undergo. Each doctor has their own methods and requirements. Before you jump into **any** surgery, it is extremely important to know your body and what is important to you. You should make a list of what you need as a result of the surgery and what you want. What are your priorities? What must you absolutely have (e.g., sensation, size, implants, etc.) to feel whole or complete, and what things are secondary or not as important.

I cannot *stress enough* that as good as the doctors are today, the end result belongs to you. It will take researching, asking questions of doctors and their patient referrals and chatting with other patients on forums to get as much information as possible.[23] Education! Education! Education!

Gender-affirming surgeries for trans women.

Chances are, if you have been on puberty-blockers, most if not all of the secondary natal male characteristics may not develop and you will probably not need ***facial***

23 See *Appendix VI* for a great place to start.

feminization surgery (FFS.) If not, many women, (though by no means all), get FFS to give their face's bone structure a "softer" impression. They are medically necessary because they increase the likelihood of trans women being recognized as female and help them avoid harassment.

FFS includes various types of plastic surgery alterations:

- The chin/jaw can be reshaped to have feminine features.
- Cheeks/lips can be resized to be larger or smaller.
- Forehead/hairline can be adjusted to create a smaller forehead and alter a masculine hairline.
- The nose can be resized and made smaller.
- Areas surrounding the eyes, ears, and mouth can be altered for a more feminine look.

Every surgeon has different techniques. It is important that you understand them and the potential risks involved. Recovery time could be as little as two weeks and as long as several months, depending on the surgical procedure(s). Some of the risks involved are:

- Infection
- Swelling
- Bruising
- Blood Loss
- Numbness
- Allergy
- Scarring

Do your homework so that you can get the most out of surgery.

Also included with FFS is a tracheal shave, which reduces the size of the throat's "Adam's apple." This is a delicate surgery where a small incision is made under the chin. The cartilage is reduced and reshaped. Initial recovery is one to two days. Your voice may be weak but it should not be long-term.

Some risks are:

- The voice may change.
- Scarring might occur.
- If the trachea is cut too deep the vocal cords could be cut, too.

This surgery barely leaves a traceable scar and the complications are usually minimal. This simple procedure can make a huge impact on trans women presenting successfully as female.

Breast augmentation is a choice of chest reconstruction for many trans women. The procedure involves using silicone or saline implants. Incisions are made around the areola (outside of nipple) and armpit to insert the implant either in front of the pectoral muscle or behind. Some alternative methods transplant fat or tissue from other parts of the body into the breast area. It's very important to wait at least a year after beginning estrogen because you could see some breast growth from the hormone treatment. Or, you may decide that you've grown as much breast tissue as possible and are ready for augmentation.

Some complications of breast augmentation to think about are:

- Silicone implants can rupture or leak, although that's less the case nowadays.
- Leaks may cause pain and lumps. If so, then removal is typically suggested to allow the tissue to heal before the surgeon tries to re-implant them.
- Leaks may travel to other parts of the body and cause pain.
- If the saline leaks, it will happen suddenly and be absorbed by the body.

Bottom surgery.

Some women have an ***orchiectomy*** to remove their testicles which produce sperm and testosterone. In doing so, testosterone suppressants (e.g., spironolactone) are no longer needed. (If you are or have been on puberty-blockers, you will not produce sperm or testosterone). Bottom surgery is not typically performed on young teens. As you get older and feel it is right for you, you should give some thought as to whether you want children in the future because once this surgery is done, it is permanent and you will not be able to have biological children.

Many women receive a ***vaginoplasty*** to create a vagina from their scrotal and penile tissue. The head of the penis and the nerves are used to form the clitoris and the scrotal tissue forms the labia and the urethra is shortened. This procedure, like all procedures, requires time to recover.

Potential complications associated with this surgery are:

- Infection
- Fistula or a small opening
- Excessive postoperative bleeding
- Necrosis (death of tissue)
- Slow healing and recovery

- Loss of sensation

Despite enduring complications sometimes, most people are satisfied with their surgical outcomes in the long-term.

Lastly, many trans women whose hairline has receded or who are balding receive a ***hair transplant***, which takes hair follicles from the side or back of the head and implants them into the bald areas.

Whether you have one surgery or many, you need to do as much research as possible so you have a clear understanding. Surgical techniques may vary. The better informed you are, the more prepared you'll be.

CHAPTER 9

Your Future

Continuing to develop yourself as a person is vital for getting through your transition successfully and preparing for life after you've transitioned—in a word, your future! While transition may feel central in your life right now, there's so much more to think about beyond transitioning. As a teen, this is an exciting time for you, because you're moving towards adulthood and getting to think about what kind of job, home, and life you want. You may even want a family someday. So you have to remember to keep your eyes on the bigger "life" picture and prevent yourself from getting bogged down in the details of transitioning and letting those issues overtake the energy you should be devoting to other areas and goals in your life.

Thinking about college or vocational school.

Are you (or were you) inspired by a particular class or subject in high school? Do you like doing physical work with your hands? Or perhaps you like creative artistic activities or working on computers? Maybe you liked some of your sciences classes? In any case, continuing your education after high school is always good.

There are lots of jobs you can begin straight out of high school. If you want to advance in a career in construction, business, art, cooking, engineering, teaching, law or healthcare, there are special vocational schools and colleges that train you in these skills and prepare you to enter the workforce. Some of them will involve earning a degree or certificate to show you've successfully acquired certain skills.

Choosing the right school can be a challenge though, and certain issues will affect your choices. Some aspiring college/vocational students pick an educational program because it looks the most interesting while others choose most affordable. Still other students pick schools/colleges based on what area of the country they want to live in. Some questions you may want to consider are: Does the school/college have a good reputation in this subject area? Can I afford the costs of tuition, books, room and board, etc.? Is there any financial aid, including grants, scholarships, or loans, that will help me with the costs? Your school guidance counselor can help you with these questions and finding the most appropriate school/college for your career interests. They can even help you fill out the application.

While these considerations are important, you should also consider whether your prospective campus is **a safe, friendly environment for LGBTQI people**. The school may have the best teachers and courses in your career field, but if you feel uncomfortable (or afraid) while being there, and no trans-related services are available, it may not be the best place for you, because feeling fearful will likely interfere with your ability to learn. Before you send out applications, do research on the social climate first to see if it's trans friendly. For example, you can comb the school/college website (or call their admissions office) for information on the school/college's policy for LGBTQI students and handling prejudice and bullying against LGBTQI students. You can also research the news for past incidents of LGBTQI harassment on the campus to get a sense of the social climate. Another suggestion is to do an Internet search for "*trans-friendly* colleges." There are also general "campus climate" surveys that include "LGBT-friendliness." But beware of these places, because a school that's open to gay, lesbian, and bisexual students may still be intolerant of trans people.

Take some time to read about what makes these colleges safe and exciting for trans students. If you know or can find some LGBTQI students who are attending (or have attended) the school/college you're interested in, consider asking them about their experiences on campus.

Questions to consider.

Does the school have an official policy of gender identity/expression nondiscrimination? Does the school have explicit rules that forbid the mistreatment of students and staff based on gender presentation or transgender identity? Do they have protocols in place to address violations of the policy, when they occur?

Does the school have an LGBTQI center? LGBTQI or trans student groups? Is there a safe space or club where trans students can gather? Does the school provide a staff member and resources to help trans students put on events? Are there any LGBTQI people on the faculty who are friendly to LGBTQI students?

Does the school have policies in place for name and gender marker changes for transgender students? Does the school's registrar or record keepers know how to change names and genders on school paperwork? Is their policy publicly available?

Does the school have gender-neutral or "all-gender" bathrooms? Does the school mark out single-stall bathrooms? Have they marked them as affirming of all genders? Do they have a list available where students can find these bathrooms?

Does the school have gender-inclusive housing? Can trans students choose what kind of housing is most comfortable for them? Can students who are transitioning while living in single-sex dormitories be housed with the gender that feels most affirming or safe? Can a trans student move out of housing if they feel unsafe? Are the resident assistants appropriately trained to handle the special needs of LGBTQI students? *Note: This is important to find out because most colleges have a mandatory policy requiring first-year students to live on campus.*

Does the school offer courses in gender, queer, and/or transgender studies? Is there a Gender or Women's Studies program or department on campus? Does your school try to integrate gender minorities in their curriculum? Are there role models for trans students and their allies among the school's staff?

Are there students available who you can talk to about your hopes and concerns? Does the school have a LGBTQI group on-campus whom you can talk with to find out the social climate on campus?

Is the school located in a trans-friendly town? Does the city or state have nondiscrimination ordinances that include protection of gender identity and/or gender expression? (Remember: Some governments have anti-discrimination laws protecting against discrimination based on sexual orientation, but not gender presentation or identity. So, be sure to find out their policies for protecting transgender people.) Are there trans- and/or queer-friendly shops, cafes, restaurants, bookstores, or "dance events," nearby that might indicate social acceptance of gender nonconforming or transgender people?

While all the schools you research may not hit every point on this list, asking these questions can help you envision what your life might be like on their campus. College isn't just about expanding your knowledge. It's about living and socializing with a new, diverse group of people. If possible, make sure this environment is set up to support rather than hinder you as you explore who you're becoming and what you want to do in life. It's very important that you take time to do research and think about the best option for your needs, because you'll be committing yourself to being there for a few years. So take your time researching and thinking.

Finding a job.

Finding the right job can be a challenge. It requires writing a resume, filling out applications, practicing for and showing up for interviews, and keeping up with your new workplace's expectations. This can be even more complicated when you're trans.

First, it's worth pointing out that your first job will likely not be the only job you will ever have. Adults, in the course of their lifetime, change jobs many times before finding the right fit. Some people even change careers from business to art, or from teaching to engineering, because they discover they have several passions.

You may take a job simply to make and save money so you can have some financial independence from your parents. There's no shame in that! Many young people work at temporary jobs to save money. Sometimes these temporary jobs can turn into a career. You might find a job through school, a temp agency, or seek out an internship related to your career interests and goals.

The big question for you is whether your employer is trans-friendly. While this may not matter to some teens, it feels essential to others. No matter how you feel about it, this is important. Find out where your potential employer stands on nondiscrimination in the workplace.

What does this mean and how can you find out?

Most employers have an employee handbook that explicitly states they will not discriminate against employees based on identifiers like race, gender, sexuality, and so on. Increasingly, gender identity and/or expression are being included in these policies, which is an indication that your boss isn't allowed to treat you differently if you are trans and/or gender-nonconforming.

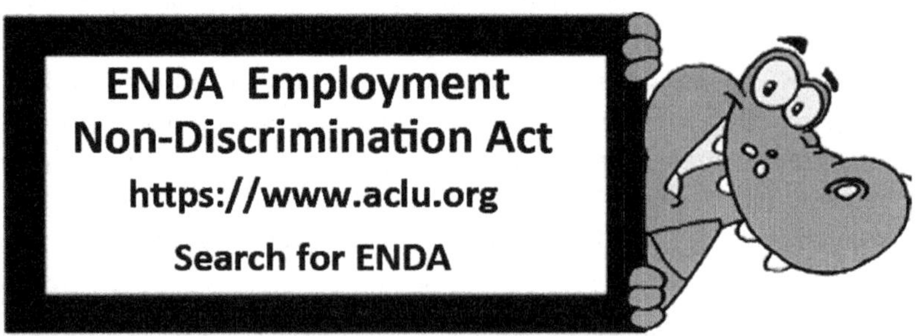

Some cities and states in the U.S. have laws that require employers to have nondiscrimination rules related to gender identity and expression. However, if you live in an area where these laws don't exist, your employer gets to decide their own policy, and they may not be up with the times or ready to acknowledge that they owe trans employees' equal treatment. Sometimes, this is just an oversight. If an employer has a rule against mistreating employees for being gay (which, in effect, means they are expressing a certain amount of "gender-nonconformity" for loving a member of the same sex), they may already be open to trans employees, too, without explicitly stating it.

Other employers feel that it is within their rights to pick on, harass, or even fire an employee for being trans or visibly gender variant. It's worth it to try to figure out ahead of time if your potential employer is one of these people. You can search their website to find information regarding their nondiscrimination practices and call anonymously to ask a representative if they have a policy in place.

For more information you can search LGBTQI organizations online to see what they say about specific companies, particularly large corporations that employ thousands of people (e.g., big chain restaurants, gas stations, and retail outlets). The Human Rights Campaign (HRC) has a Corporate Equality Index where you can search big businesses by name. The National Center for Transgender Equality (NCTE) also keeps current information on transgender people's workplace rights so you can more easily determine whether you've been discriminated against.

Another tactic you can try is searching the company's name in the "news" databases of Google to see if there are any incidents of discrimination or lawsuits in the company's history that's been reported by the media.

Being trans in the workplace.

Most trans people who are looking for a job ask themselves, *"Do I want to be 'out' about being trans or should I keep it private?"*

For many employers, your trans identity is not an issue because they're concerned with your job performance and how well you get along with other employees.

It's realistic to acknowledge that we live in a world where disclosing one's trans status can still, depending on where you live, prejudice an employer against hiring you, set you up for possible mistreatment, and even lead to your being fired. Even if you're in an area where this treatment is technically against the law, you may feel like you have to put up with it in order to keep your job. Others in the same situation file lawsuits, which can be a daunting experience in itself.

While you may feel good about being trans and want to share your trans history with other people in your life, you might also feel a unique pressure to keep it under wraps at work or while you're searching for a job. Do what you have to do to survive. You may find it feels safe to come out in the workplace after being there for a while and getting to know your co-workers and boss. I know many men and women who come out privately to a handful of coworkers and remain *"stealth"* (non-disclosing) to the rest of the company. But be careful doing that, because even the most trusted confidants in your circle can still spill the beans because it feels like a "big secret," even though it shouldn't be.

Workplaces throw us into a diverse group of people and situations that can be both exciting and stressful. As you enter the workforce, you'll likely encounter bosses or coworkers, who have political, social, or religious beliefs that differ from yours. By using your best judgement, you will learn how to navigate the larger world of different perspectives.

Here are some additional questions you may want to consider when dealing with an employer.

Should I come out as trans to my prospective employer during an interview?

This is a deeply personal decision and one that relies on context. First ask yourself:

- *Am I in an interview environment where I feel safe?*
- *Do I know whether this employer has a nondiscrimination policy in place?*
- *Do I get the sense that this is an open, affirming work environment or one where people don't talk very much about their personal lives?*

Trust your gut intuition and remember that it's never a requirement that you have to tell a prospective employer about your trans identity. There's no law that says you have to disclose. It's simply a part of your personal history and has no bearing on whether you can be a good worker or not.

In fact, throwing in personal details during interviews can be awkward and uncomfortable sometimes, so I recommend that you focus on highlighting your passion and skills that match the job requirements. If you're trying to ascertain whether the company is trans-friendly, the interview *is not* the best place to test the waters.

My legal ID still lists my birth gender, but I want to fill out the application's "M or F" question with my true gender. Will I get in trouble with my prospective employer?

It is not illegal to list a different gender on a job application than the one on your driver's license, social security card, or birth certificate. Over time, we fill out an **"M"** or **"F"** on so many different applications and documents that most trans people find that the paper trails of their gender marker are a jumble. That's totally okay.[24]

In theory, you shouldn't get into any "trouble" for having a gender mis-match on your records. However, if you have chosen to keep quiet about your trans identity at work and an employer notices this discrepancy, they may ask you about it at some point. So think ahead and be prepared with some answers in case it comes up.

Some people find it easier to just "laugh off" and downplay the incorrect gender marker on their legal ID. Others decide that this is the best moment to come out as trans at work. If your workplace has a nondiscrimination policy in place, this should not result in you being fired (even if the conversation might be awkward). If they do not, then coming out could result in you losing the job.

Knowing this, you may decide to *"control"* the coming out situation by doing it yourself, before anyone else "discovers" it about you. This strategy helps you "get out in front" of the narrative that others might spin about you and manage the way people receive the information. In short, it's a way to shape their perceptions of you before others can paint "the" picture.

What can I do if I'm being harassed or treated unfairly for being trans?

If you feel you are being mistreated at work, which can include being the target of teasing or hateful comments, being sexually harassed, being mis-gendered with

24 Check here for all your rights: http://transequality.org/know-your-rights/

incorrect pronouns or names, being barred from using the correct bathroom, being treated differently from your co-workers (e.g., receiving excessive or inadequate amounts of work), or being demoted or looked over for promotions because you're trans, then the first step you need to take is to start documenting each instance of discrimination.

Keep an ongoing journal where you record the date, time, witnesses, and nature of each instance of mistreatment.

Also keep track of when you spoke to management about the offense and their response. When you're compiling your record, be careful to assess whether each situation is genuine discrimination based on being trans. Usually our suspicions are correct, but there are some instances where we might misread a situation that is hurtful, but it's more because of ignorance than prejudice. Often, people who are struggling to understand their trans coworker make off-color remarks to assess yours and others' reactions, but it does not become a pattern of behavior. Sometimes people are awkward, misinformed, or regularly fumble with pronouns/name, and they should be corrected by you or an ally. It only becomes discrimination when you have corrected their behavior and it still persists, or humiliates or makes you feel unsafe.

Once you're confident that you're facing trans discrimination, and have a record of examples and witnesses, plan how you will talk to management. If you're at a job that has a human resources department this means that you have a representative whose job is to act as a "go between" and take your concerns to management. They can help you form a plan of action about how to talk to your coworkers, too. If you don't have a "middleman" to represent you, plan how you will sit down with your boss.

Your boss may acknowledge the discrimination and tell you that it will stop, or they may deny it entirely. Remain calm and professional regardless of their response and consider how it will affect your next move. If they tell you the mistreatment will stop, ask them how they plan to intervene and stop the behavior. If they are nonchalant about your complaints and don't appear to take you seriously then, you have some choices. You can try to ignore the people who are mistreating you, or you may be able to talk to them. Keep in mind that, talking to these people may or may not change their attitudes and antics towards you, and it could create more distress, because, if they're mistreating you in the first place, that's a good indication of just how deeply they're entrenched in anti-trans bias and don't want to change. You can choose to quit the job and look for another one in a work setting that's more supportive, or you can look for legal counsel to possibly take action against your employer(s), if they are violating a nondiscrimination law. Maybe you feel that it's important to hold your company accountable by continuing to file complaints and maybe even getting a lawyer involved. At the end of the day, only you can make that decision.

Keep in mind that currently in the U.S., there is no federal or nation-wide law that fully protects transgender people from discrimination in the workplace, so you should research the laws in your city and state by going to sources like Lambda Legal, Human Rights Campaign, and the federal government's Employment Opportunity Commission. *(See Appendix III.)*

Ultimately, there's no single right way to address workplace discrimination. Again, it's all about your safety. Maybe survival is the most important thing for you right now, so you choose to stay in a less-than-healthy workplace and find ways in the meantime to care for yourself outside of work (e.g., talking to friends, therapy, releasing stress through exercise, or artistic expression). You may feel the situation is too intolerable and that it's best for you to simply move on to another job. If possible, and your safety and sanity aren't in danger, try to secure another job before quitting the current one.

Many trans activists are working hard to change discrimination laws and increase workplace protections for trans people. With increasing rights for trans people, employers are beginning to see that what matters most is not their employees' gender identity or expression, but how well they perform their job.

Finding yourself, finding your purpose: happiness as you grow older.

While middle school or high school may feel a little overwhelming right now, it's only a small fraction of your life in the larger scheme of things. You'll be graduating soon, and you'll have plenty of space and time to figure out what you really want out of this crazy thing called life.

Leaving high school (and perhaps your parents' home) is a thrilling and frightening leap into independence. It's up to you to remain positive and healthy. It's easy, as a young adult, to get wrapped up in other people (friends or lovers), partying, working or activism. The key to staying sane and stable is to *balance your energy* between your job, family, community, and yourself.

Adults still face peer pressure and so will you. Adults face temptations to engage in excessive drinking or use illicit drugs. Adults who've faced abuse as youth can sometimes perpetuate those behaviors in their own relationships if they're not careful. Adults still need to plan for the long haul by saving money and building lasting relationships with family, friends, and community.

A lot of time our intuition can lead us in the right direction. So listen to your gut and your heart. Spend as much time as you can around people who are positive and who truly appreciate you. If you follow the toolkit of character building in this book, you'll be well equipped to handle the beautiful journey of life.

I wish you all the best as you grow "alligator skin" and continue down your path. Be well.

APPENDICES

APPENDIX I
TERMINOLOGY

The terminology below is compiled from: http://www.transactiveonline.org/index.php and http://transhealth.vch.ca/

Like any marginalized group, the lives of transgender people are rife with phrases and terms that may not be familiar to non-transgender people. These definitions may help you better understand and communicate in a respectful and accurate way on transgender issues and experiences. Some of these terms are no longer used, and terminology is also changing frequently. New terms will also appear in the future.

AFAB/FAAB: Abbreviation for Assigned Female At Birth or Female Assigned At Birth. Refers to the assigned gender role a person is given at birth. Some trans people use them to describe their gender history. They also help people who do not want to be pinned down to an essentialist narrative about their sex.

AMAB/MAAB: Abbreviation for Assigned-Male-At-Birth or Male-Assigned-At-Birth. See above for further definition.

Affirmed Female: Someone with a female gender identity who was assigned male at birth. This is more accurate and respectful than some alternate descriptors like male-to-female, because it characterizes her transition as affirming the gender she knows herself to be, rather than changing from one gender to another.

Affirmed Male: Someone with a male gender identity who assigned female at birth. This is more accurate and respectful than some alternate descriptors like female-to-male, because it characterizes his transition as affirming the gender he knows himself to be, rather than changing from one gender to another

Agender: Some agender people define their identity as being neither a man nor a woman while others would define agender as not having any gender.

Ally: A cis-gender person who supports and celebrates trans identities, challenges transphobia, and explores these biases in themselves.

Androgynous: A blend of masculinity and femininity gender. Someone identifying as androgynous might refer to themselves as an androgyne.

Assigned Gender Role: Our social status as a boy, girl, man or woman—correlated to our birth sex. Includes a shifting set of masculine or feminine stereotypes, behaviors or interests that an individual is expected to conform to. This can be particularly problematic for transgender people.

Assigned Sex/Birth Sex: Birth sex is defined exclusively as male, female or intersex. This is most commonly established by a prenatal ultrasound or postnatal external examination at birth, though intersexuality may not become apparent until adolescence or later.

Assigned Sex: Refers to a (discredited) medical practice in which an intersex infant with ambiguous genitalia is surgically altered to conform to a more typical male or female appearance and subsequently expected to live in the gender role associated with their altered genitalia.

Bigender/Trigender/Pangender: People who feel they are two, three, or more genders. They may shift between genders or identify as all of them at the same time.

Binarism: Intolerance towards people who identify outside of the gender binary (man/woman). The belief that man/woman are the only legitimate genders.

Binding: Compressing one's chest to create a more androgynous or masculine appearance.

Boi: A term used in a variety of ways. Generally, boi conveys a level of identification with maleness and/or masculinity. However, the versatility of the word means this isn't always the case.

Black Market Hormones: Hormones purchased without a prescription.

Blockers/Pubertal Suppression/Puberty Blockers: Puberty delaying medical interventions (GnRH analogues) designed to relieve the psychological trauma and unwanted physical changes associated with wrong-gender pubertal development in trans adolescents. The treatment allows trans youth time to actively participate, via informed consent, in their medical care. Initiated at or after Tanner Stage 2 and often prior to the administration of cross sex hormones (estrogen, progesterone, testosterone, etc.).

Bottom Surgery: A variety of gender related genital surgeries, including:

vaginoplasty, phalloplasty, vaginectomy, metoidioplasty, orchiectomy, clitoroplasty, scrotoplasty, and others.

Breast Augmentation: A gender-affirming, feminizing, top surgery that enlarges one's breasts.

Butch/Femme: Adjectives used to describe one's gender expression characteristics. A masculine-spectrum person (of any gender) might be described as butch; a feminine-spectrum person (of any gender) might be described as femme. Butch and Femme can also be gender identities unto themselves.

CAFAB: Acronym for Coercively Assigned Female at Birth; refers to people declared to be female at birth and raised in a female gender role that does not match their gender identity.

CAMAB: Acronym for Coercively Assigned Male at Birth; refers to people declared to be male at birth and raised in a male gender role that does not match their gender identity.

Canadian Professional Association for Transgender Health (CPATH): Professional organization devoted to trans health, whose mission as an international multidisciplinary professional association is to promote evidence based care, education, research, advocacy, public policy and respect in trans health.

Chest Surgery: A gender-affirming, masculinizing, top surgery that removes breast tissue and sculpts remaining tissue into a shape that is typically considered to be more masculine.

Cis-gender: Someone whose gender identity matches the gender role they were assigned at birth; a person who is not trans. The Latin prefix "cis'" means "on the same side of." Cis-gender is preferable to "biological" or "genetic" male or female.

Cis-gender Privilege: The privileges cis-gender people have because their gender identity matches their assigned gender role and because they are considered "normal." For example, cis-gender people don't have to worry about violence and institutionalized discrimination because they identify with a gender that's different from their assigned birth gender.

Cissexism/Cis-gender Supremacy: The institutional and societal marginalization of trans people; expressing hate and bigotry toward trans people.

Cissexual: Sometimes this term is used synonymously with cis-gender. See cis-gender definition.

Clitoralplasty: Part of vaginoplasty surgery in which the clitoris is created from a small section of the head of the penis.

Clitoral Release: A gender-affirming, masculinizing, lower surgery that cuts ligaments below the clitoris to release it from the pubis and expose the shaft more.

Colpocleisis: A procedure that closes the vagina by suturing the walls together. Colpocleisis is largely irreversible.

Coming Out: The process of becoming aware of one's LGBTQI identity, accepting it, and/or telling others about it.

Cross Dresser: People who wear clothing associated with a different gender than the gender they were assigned at birth. Cross-dressers may or may not identify as trans. The term replaced "transvestite," which is now considered offensive by many people.

Cross-Sex Hormones/Hormone Replacement Therapy (HRT): Refers to treatment that can include, but is not limited to the following hormonal interventions: estrogen ("E"), testosterone ("T"), progesterone, estrogen suppressants, testosterone suppressants, etc.

Detransition: To reverse some (or all) of the physical and social changes that a person underwent to alter their body to fit their gender identity. Some people return to their birth assigned gender, while others detransition to another gender.

Disorders of Sex Development (DSD): A reproductive or sexual anatomy that does not closely resemble typical male or female reproductive or sexual anatomy, which may include genitalia, secondary sex characteristics, and/or chromosomal make-up. DSD replaced terms like "hermaphrodite." DSD is different from trans.

Drag: Taking on the appearance and characteristics associated with a certain gender, usually for entertainment and often to expose the humorous elements of gender.

Drag King/Queen: Performance artists who dress and act in a masculine or feminine manner to parody male or female gender stereotypes as part of their routine. Might identify as trans, but not necessarily.

Endocrinologist: A doctor with special training in the study of hormones and their actions and disorders in the body.

Facial feminization surgery: Surgeries that feminize the face, including tracheal (Adam's apple) reduction, nose feminization, facial bone reduction, face lift, eyelid rejuvenation, and hair reconstruction.

Female: A sex assigned at birth based on chromosomes (e.g., XX), gene expression, hormone levels and function, and reproductive/sexual anatomy (e.g., vagina, uterus).

FTM/F2M/Female-to-Male: Refers to someone with a female birth sex and assigned gender role who identifies as male. While still commonly used, the term is becoming outdated and used less frequently than "affirmed male."

Feminine: Describes socially and culturally constructed aspects of gender (e.g., roles, behavior, expression, identity) typically associated with girls and women.

Feminizing Hormone Therapy: The use of medications (e.g., estrogen, anti-androgens, progestins) to develop physical characteristics that are in line with one's gender identity or gender expression, including breast development, fat distribution on the hips, thighs, and buttocks, and softer skin.

Feminizing Surgeries: Gender-affirming surgical procedures that create physical characteristics reflective of one's gender identity and/or gender expression, including breast augmentation, vaginoplasty, facial feminization surgery, voice surgery, thyroid cartilage reduction, buttock augmentation/lipofilling, and hair reconstruction.

Femme: Describes gender expressions and/or social and relationship roles that are perceived as feminine, or a person who embodies these qualities. Might identify as trans, but not necessarily.

"Full-Time": Slang term for living the identity and roles associated with one's preferred gender all the time. While this term is being replaced by the saying, "I've transitioned," it's still used by some trans people.

Gaff: A garment that conceals the penis and testes by flattening them.

Gay/Straight Alliance (GSA): Student-led organizations that provide a safe and supportive environment for LGBTQI and questioning youth and their allies. See also QSA.

Gender: The experience of being male, female, both or neither in any combination. Gender is a spectrum, not a binary. While gender stereotypes are most certainly a social construct, the self-experience of gender is innate and unique to every individual.

Gender Binary: The pervasive social system telling us there can only be masculine men and feminine women with no alternatives or diversity of gender identity or expression.

Gender Confirming Surgery (GCS)/Sex Reassignment Surgery (SRS)/ Gender Affirming Surgery: Includes a broad range of surgical procedures trans people may undergo to align their bodies with their gender identity.

Gender Creative: Refers to people who identify and express their gender differently from societal expectations.

Gender Diverse: Gender roles and/or expressions that don't conform to social and cultural expectations; gender non-conforming.

Gender Dysphoria: Gender dysphoria is a feeling of unhappiness or discomfort with some or all gendered aspects of one's body, or in response to social mis-gendering. Most trans people experience gender dysphoria at some point in their lives, although it's not a constant state and can be relieved (or eliminated) by transitioning.

Gender Expression: How we express ourselves personally and socially according to gender mores and roles. There is no right or wrong way to express gender, but gender nonconformity is often seen as a social transgression.

Gender Fluid: Someone whose gender identity or expression may vary from day to day or for whom gender identity/expression isn't fixed on a permanent basis.

Gender Identity: How we understand and experience our gender. One's gender identity may or may not align with their assigned gender role

Gender-inclusive/Neutral Pronouns: Pronouns used to avoid gender binary-based references such as she/her, he/him, ze/hir or they/them.

Gender Nonconforming/GNC: Not fully conforming to the social expectations of one's assigned gender in terms of identity, expression, roles, or performance.

Gender Normative: Gender roles and/or expressions that match social and cultural expectations.

Genderqueer: An umbrella term referring to gender nonconforming non-binary people.

Gender Questioning: Someone who's evaluating their gender identity and expression.

Gender Role: Social expectations of how people should act, feel, and express themselves based on their gender.

Getting "Read": Also known as getting "clocked." When someone identifies an individual as trans; can lead to misgendering and dangerous (even life threatening) in some situations;

Hair Restoration Surgery: Surgical technique that moves individual hair follicles from one part of the body to another part, usually the scalp.

Hermaphrodite: An outdated term that was used historically to label people with a reproductive anatomy that's a combination of elements (genitalia, gonads, sex chromosomes) of typical male and female system This term has been replaced by the more respectful term, "disorders of sex development" or DSD.

Homosexual: An outdated term used historically to describe people who are attracted to people in their own gender group. This term has been replaced by "gay" or "lesbian."

Hormone Therapy (HT): Administration of sex hormones to bring one's secondary sex characteristics more in line with one's gender identity; hormone replacement therapy; HRT; trans hormonal therapy.

Hormone Readiness Assessment: Evaluation conducted by a healthcare professional to determine if a patient is ready to begin hormone therapy.

Hysterectomy: A surgical procedure to remove all or part of the uterus, and sometimes the ovaries and/or fallopian tubes; a gender-affirming, masculinizing lower surgery.

Intersex: A general term used for a variety of conditions in which a person is born with a reproductive or sexual anatomy that doesn't seem to fit the typical definitions of female or male. While trans and intersex are not synonymous or interchangeable terms, some intersex people also identify trans.

Lifestyle choice: An outdated and offensive term used to imply that trans people make a choice in the way that they live their lives or behave in ways that are according to the attitudes, tastes, and values associated with the gender identity.

Lipofilling: The surgical transfer of fat removed by liposuction to other areas of the body.

Liposuction: A surgical technique for removing excess fat from under the skin by suction.

Lo-Ho: A slang term used by some trans people who take low doses of hormones.

Lower Surgery: Umbrella term for gender-affirming surgeries done below the waist, including masculinizing (e.g., hysterectomy, clitoral release, metoidioplasty, and phalloplasty) and feminizing (e.g., orchiectomy and vaginoplasty) surgeries. Also called "bottom surgery."

LGBT: Acronym for Lesbian, Gay, Bisexual, and Trans people; GLBT.

LGBT2Q: An evolving acronym for Lesbian, Gay, Bisexual, Trans, Two-Spirit, Queer, and additional identities.

LGBTQI: An evolving acronym for Lesbian, Gay, Bisexual, Trans, Queer, Intersex

Male: A sex, usually assigned at birth, and based on chromosomes (e.g., XY), gene expression, hormone levels and function, and reproductive/sexual anatomy (e.g., penis, testicles).

MTF/M2F/Male-to-Female: Refers to someone with a male birth sex and assigned gender role but who identifies as female. While still commonly used, it is considered a less than accurate and/or respectful description of a transgender girl/woman. This term puts the emphasis on changing a physical state or becoming something "other" than what you already are. *(See Affirmed Female above)*

Man: A human being who self-identifies as a man, based on elements of importance to the individual, such as gender roles, behavior, expression, identity, and/or physiology.

Masculine: Describes socially and culturally constructed aspects of gender (e.g., roles, behavior, expression, identity) typically associated with boys and men.

Masculinizing Hormone Therapy: The use of testosterone to develop physical characteristics that are in line with one's gender identity or gender expression, including more facial hair, more body hair, increased muscle mass, and deepened voice.

Masculinizing Surgeries: Gender-affirming surgical procedures that create physical characteristics reflective of one's gender identity and/or gender expression, including chest surgery, hysterectomy, clitoral release, metoidioplasty, phalloplasty, pectoral implants, liposuction, and lipofilling.

Medical Transition: To undergo medical steps one deems necessary to transition to one's preferred sex, for example hormones therapy and/or gender affirming surgery.

Metoidioplasty: A gender-affirming, masculinizing, lower surgery to create a penis and scrotum, done by cutting ligaments around the clitoris to add length to the shaft, grafting skin around the shaft to create added girth, lengthening the urethra so one can urinate from the shaft, and creating a scrotum.

Monthly Bleeding: A term for "menstrual bleeding" or "period" used by some trans people.

No-Ho: A slang term used by some trans people who do not take hormones.

Non-flesh penis: Penis made from synthetic materials; may also be referred to as a "packer" or "prosthetic penis."

Non-Op: Short for **Non-Operative**. Someone who, for medical reasons or personal choice, does not plan to undergo Gender Confirmation Surgery (GCS).

Oophorectomy: A surgery to remove the ovaries; a gender-affirming, masculinizing lower surgery.

Orchiectomy: A surgery to remove the testicles; a gender-affirming, feminizing, lower surgery.

"Outing": To reveal to others a previously unknown aspect of someone's identity without that individual's prior permission; usually applies to gender identity or sexual orientation.

Packing: A term some people use to describe wearing padding or a non-flesh penis in the front of the lower garment or underwear.

Padding: Use of undergarments to create the appearance of larger breasts, hips, and/or buttocks. Includes breast forms.

Pangender: Gender identity that includes all genders; multi-gender; omni-gender.

"Passing": Integrating successfully in social settings as one's experienced gender without question or incident by others. It is a negative term as it implies that one is "pretending" to be something they are not, or are, to some extent, "fooling people." It is just better to say that we are being recognized as a man or woman

Penis*: Penis* (with an asterisk) is used to acknowledge the many different words that are used for this body part: penis, strapless, shenis, etc.

Person of Trans History: Someone who has transitioned to female or transitioned to male and no longer identifies as trans.

Phalloplasty: A gender-affirming, masculinizing, lower surgery to create a penis and scrotal sac (phase 1), then testicular implants and implants to obtain rigidity/ erection (phases 2 and 3). This surgery is performed differently by each surgeon.

Preferred Pronoun: The pronouns an individual prefers to have used in reference to them, such as she or he, they, ze, or the person's name.

Pre-Op: Short for Pre-Operative. Someone who has not yet had GCS, but who intends to undergo such surgery.

Post-Op: Short for Post-Operative. Refers to someone who has undergone GCS.

Primary Care Provider: An individual's main health care provider in non-emergency situations (checkups, referrals); Family Doctor; General Practitioner (GP); Nurse Practitioner (NP).

Privilege: Refers to the social, economic and political advantages and power held by people from dominant groups on the basis of attributes such as gender, race, sexual orientation, and social class.

Queer/Straight Alliance (QSA): Student-led organizations intended to provide a safe and supportive environment for lesbian, gay, bisexual, trans, Two-Spirit, and queer/questioning youth and their allies; see also GSA.

Questioning: A term sometimes used by those in the process of exploring their gender identity or sexual orientation, as well as choosing not to identify with any other label.

QTPOC: Acronym for Queer, Trans, and People of Color.

QTIPOC: Acronym for Queer, Trans, and Indigenous People of Color.

Read as: When someone is correctly assumed to be the gender that they identify as; this term has replaced the outdated term "to pass" which implied that a person is failing when they are not being read as the gender that they identify as.

Recognized: Someone who is just seen as man or woman (same as READ AS). Better than "passing."

Real Life Experience (RLE): A former requirement for medical transition, during which one was required to live full-time in their self-determined gender role; this requirement has been removed in the current WPATH Standards of Care (Version 7).

Salpingectomy: A surgery to remove the Fallopian tubes; a gender-affirming, masculinizing lower surgery.

Scrotoplasty: Procedure that creates scrotum for testicular implants out of native labial tissue.

Self-Identified Men: Term used to be inclusive of trans men or trans persons of history who self-identity as men (e.g., this restroom is for self-identified men).

Self-Identified Women: Term used to be inclusive of trans women or trans persons of history who self-identity as women.

Sex: Biological attributes and legal categories used to classify humans as male, female, intersex or other categories, primarily associated with physical and physiological features including chromosomes, genetic expression, hormone levels and function, and reproductive/sexual anatomy.

Sex Assignment: Legal designation of sex assigned at birth.

Sexual Orientation: an enduring personal quality that inclines people to feel romantic or sexual attraction (or a combination of these) to persons of another sex or gender, the same sex or gender, or to multiple sexes or more than one gender.

- NOTE: Gender Identity and Sexual Orientation are developmentally different and they occur at different stages in the maturation process.

Sex Hormones: Hormones, such as estrogen and testosterone, affecting sexual and reproductive development or function.

Sex Marker: Legal designation of sex (usually male or female) on official documents, such as government issued identification and birth certificates. Sometimes called "gender marker."

Sex Reassignment Surgery: See gender-affirming surgery.

Standards of Care (for the Health of Transsexual, Transgender and Gender Non-Conforming People): Guidelines containing the recommended course of care for people seeking medical transition to their self-determined gender, published by the World Professional Association for Transgender Health (WPATH.ORG)

Stand-to-Pee/STP: A device that allows individuals to urinate standing up.

"Stealth": A slang term within transgender culture for someone who has made a conscious decision to not reveal or share their transgender history with others. The option of choosing to be "stealth" requires, to some extent, the ability to integrate successfully in social settings (see "passing" above). While making the choice to not reveal one's transgender history is a matter of personal privacy, the use of the term "stealth" can be misunderstood to mean sneaking or spying in some way.

Surgical Readiness Assessment: Evaluation conducted by a healthcare professional to determine if a patient is ready to be referred for gender-affirming surgery.

Tanner Stages: A scale of physical development in children, adolescents and adults. The scale defines pubertal changes based on external primary and secondary sex characteristics, such as the size of the breasts, genitalia, testicular volume and development of pubic and axillary hair. Tanner 1 is pre-pubertal, Tanner 2-4 is pubertal and Tanner 5 is adult maturation of secondary sex characteristics. Due to natural variation, individuals pass through the Tanner stages at different rates, depending in particular on the timing of puberty.

Third Gender: A gender other than male or female.

Total Laparoscopic Hysterectomy (TLH): Removal of cervix, uterus, ovaries and fallopian tubes (everything); minimally invasive, shorter recovery.

Top Surgery: Refers to removal of breast tissue in order to create male chest contours. Puberty suppression at the onset of adolescence followed by cross-sex hormone therapy can eliminate the need for these procedures in transgender males. The term can also apply to breast augmentation surgery for transgender females, though it is most commonly used in relation to transgender males.

TPOC: An acronym for Trans People of Color.

Trans (Trans, Transgender, Transsexual): Trans is an umbrella term that describes a wide range of people whose gender identity and/or gender expression differ from their assigned sex and/or the societal and cultural expectations of their assigned sex; includes people who identify as androgyne, agender, bigender, butch, CAFAB, CAMAB, cross-dresser, drag king, drag queen, femme, FTM, gender creative, gender fluid, gender non-conforming, genderqueer, gender variant, MTF, pangender, questioning, trans, trans man, trans woman, transfeminine, transgender, transmasucline, transsexual, and two-spirit.

Transfeminine: This umbrella term may describe people who were assigned male at birth, who identify as trans, and whose gender expression leans towards the feminine.

Transgender/TG: An umbrella term that encompasses a person or persons who, in one way or another, transcend their assigned gender role. Transgender is an adjective, not a noun, and can refer to both an individual and group: "I am transgender," "She is transgender," "All the youth in that group are transgender."

Transition: Transition is an individual process and can mean a lot of things, but a broad definition is the process transgender people may go through to align their body with their gender identity. Transitioning may include social, physical, mental, and emotional components and may not fit into the narrative we are used to seeing. Transition may or may not include things like changing one's name, having puberty suppressed, cross-sex hormone therapy, undergoing surgery, changing legal documents, coming out to loved ones, and dressing as one chooses

Trans man: May describe someone who identifies as trans and a man.

Transmasculine: This umbrella term may describe people who were assigned female at birth, who identify as trans, and whose gender expression leans towards the masculine.

Trans-misogyny: Transphobia directed at trans women and transfeminine people that reinforces male power and privilege, including harassment, violence and discrimination.

Transphobia: Ignorance, fear, dislike, and/or hatred of trans people, which may be expressed through name-calling, disparaging jokes, exclusion, rejection, harassment, violence, and many forms of discrimination (refusing to use a person's name/pronoun, denial of services, employment, housing).

Transvestite: An outdated term that was historically used to label people who cross dressed as having a mental illness; replaced by the more inclusive and respectful term, "cross dresser," which is not considered a mental illness.

Trans Woman: May describe someone who identifies as trans and a woman.

Two-Spirit: A term specific to Native American/First Nations people who are a blend of masculinity and femininity. Some non-Native American gender nonconforming people have adopted it as descriptive of their own gender experience.

"Tucking": The process of folding the penis back between the legs and concealing the testicles by pushing them back up into the inguinal canal. This is done to create a more typical female contour in the genital area.

Vagina*: Vagina* (with an asterisk) is used to acknowledge the many different words that are used for this body part: front hole, etc.

Vaginectomy: See colpoclesis.

Vaginoplasty: A gender-affirming, feminizing, lower surgery to create a vagina and vulva (including mons, labia, clitoris, and urethral opening) by inverting the penis, scrotal sac and testes.

Vocal feminization surgery: Feminizing surgery to elevate the pitch of the voice.

Woman: A human being who self-identifies as a woman, based on elements of importance to the individual, such as gender roles, behavior, expression, identity, and/or physiology.

World Professional Association for Transgender Health (WPATH): Professional organization devoted to transgender health, whose mission as an international multidisciplinary professional association is to promote evidence based care, education, research, advocacy, public policy, and respect in transgender health.

Ze/Hir: Gender-inclusive pronouns used to avoid gender binary based words (he/she, him/her), or making assumptions about other people's gender.

APPENDIX II
SUPPORT SERVICES

Some of the websites listed below do not mention *"trans"* in their title, but they support trans youth nonetheless.

Campus Pride (RANKING COLLEGES on their LGBTQI support) http://www.campuspride.org/

College Fair

http://glsen.org/article/campus-pride-and-glsen-partner-college-fairs

Gay, Lesbian, and Straight Education Network (GLSEN)

http://glsen.org/

Gay/Straight Alliance Network

http://www.gsanetwork.org/

Gender Identity Project at the NYC LGBTQI Center https://gaycenter.org/wellness/gender-identity

Los Angeles Gay & Lesbian Center's Transgender Economic Empowerment Project

http://www.weho.org/services/social-services/social-service-agency-profiles/transgender-economic-empowerment-project-la-gay-lesbian-center

Los Angeles LGBTQI Center

http://www.lalgbtcenter.org/youth_center

PFLAG (Parents, Families, Friends and Allies United with LGBTQI People to move equality forward)

http://community.pflag.org/staff/transgender

http://community.pflag.org/

The Trevor Project

http://www.thetrevorproject.org/section/get-help

TransLife Center at Chicago House

http://www.chicagohouse.org/?post_causes=translife-center

Trans Student Educational Resources

http://transstudent.org/

Trans Youth Family Allies

http://www.imatyfa.org/

Trans Youth Support Network

http://www.transyouthsupportnetwork.org/

UCLA Trans Resources

http://www.lgbt.ucla.edu/transresources.html

PERSAD Pennsylvania

https://persadcenter.org/pages/transgender-services

HOTLINES

TransLifeline (Suicide Hotline)

http://www.translifeline.org/

Hotline for Teens

http://www.glnh.org/talkline/

National Domestic Violence Hotline

1-800-799-7233

National Teen Dating Abuse Hotline

1-866-331-9474

Appendix III
Advocacy and Legal Services

ENDA

https://www.aclu.org/hiv-aids_lgbt-rights/employment-non-discrimination-act

Gay and Lesbian Advocates and Defenders

http://www.glad.org/

Human Rights Campaign

http://www.hrc.org/topics/transgender

Lambda Legal

http://www.lambdalegal.org/

National Center for Lesbian Rights

http://www.nclrights.org/explore-the-issues/transgender-law/

National Center for Transgender Equality

http://transequality.org/

National LGBTQI Task Force

http://www.thetaskforce.org/

Sylvia Rivera Law Project

http://srlp.org/

Title IX

https://www.aclu.org/blog/victory-title-ix-protects-transgender-students

http://www.justice.gov/crt/about/cor/coord/titleix.php

http://www2.ed.gov/about/offices/list/ocr/docs/qa-201404-title-ix.pdf

Task Force, Transgender Civil Rights Project

http://www.thetaskforce.org/tcrp/

Transgender Law Center

http://transgenderlawcenter.org/

Trans Justice at the Audre Lorde Project

http://alp.org/

Trans People of Color Coalition

http://www.transpoc.org/

Transgender Legal Defense and Education Fund

http://www.transgenderlegal.org/

APPENDIX IV
INFORMATIONAL WEBSITES

Art of Transliness

http://theartoftransliness.com/

FTMGuide HUDSONS

http://www.ftmguide.org/

Gendered Intelligence

http://genderedintelligence.co.uk/

GLAAD Transgender Media and Education Program

http://www.glaad.org/transgender

I AM: Trans People Speak Project

http://www.transpeoplespeak.org/

Laura's Playground

http://www.lauras-playground.com/oddcast.htm

Neutrois Nonsense

http://neutrois.me/

Susan's Place

http://www.susans.org/

The Trans 100

http://thetrans100.com/

Tips for Trans Folk

http://tipsfortransfolk.tumblr.com/

TransGuys.com

http://transguys.com/

Trans Media Watch U.K.

http://www.transmediawatch.org/index.html

We Happy Trans

http://wehappytrans.com/

Female to Male

http://www.femaletomale.org/

Name Change Information

http://www.tsroadmap/reality/name-change.html

(Check your county/state for specific information regarding name change because they vary from state to state. Remember that requirements also change.)

Gender Marker on Driver's License

http://www.thetranstionalmale.com/dlchange

(Check your county/state for specific information regarding name change because they vary from state to state. Remember that requirements also change.)

Social Security

http://www.transequality.org/Resources/SSAResource_June2013.pdf

Passport

http:// www.transequality.org/Resources/Resources/passports_2012.pdf

(You cannot switch gender markers on an old passport. If you have a passport, you will have to file for a new one because you are considered a new person.)

Travel

http://travel.state.gov/content/passports/english/go/lgbt.html

Nearest Passport Facility

http://iafdb.travel.state.gov/

Gender Change

http://travel.state.gov/content/passports/english/passports/information/gender.html

MTF CLOTHING AND SELF-PRESENTATION

The following websites can help you get started. There are others you can google. Use common sense when listening to them.

Glamour Boutique

http://www.glamourboutique.com/

Janet's Closet

https://www.janetscloset.com/index.php

Lingerie Talk

http://www.lingerietalk.com/2012/03/26/lingerie-news/were-done-hiding-a-first-lingerie-line-for-transgendered-women.html

Size Conversion Chart

http://www.susans.org/reference/size.html

Dressing Tips

https://www.youtube.com/watch?v=p70B93DFd10

MTF Tips

https://www.youtube.com/channel/UCTGkVAKu9yYvWdylBfTxbig

Makeup Secrets

https://www.youtube.com/watch?v=T2KVBpLm30c

Female Voice

https://www.youtube.com/watch?v=a02_j7PGTPI

Transgender Care

http://www.transgendercare.com

Gaff

http://www.thebreastformstore.com/mens-gaffs2.aspx

FTM CLOTHES

Clothes

Tranzwear

http://www.tranzwear.net/

How a Suit Should Fit

http://www.artofmanliness.com/2013/09/25/good-fitted-suit-visual/

Tall Men's Shoes

http://www.tallmenshoes.com/

Short Men Styles

http://www.shortmenstyle.com/

Binders

Boxers and Binders

http://boxersandbinders.com/

T-Kingdom

http://www.t-kingdom.com/

Underworks

http://www.underworks.com/tri-top-chest-binder

In a Bind

https://www.transactiveonline.org/inabind/faqs.php

GC2b

http://www.gc2b.co/

F2mbinders

http://www.f2mbinders.com/

Big Brother Binder Program

https://www.facebook.com/pages/Big-Brothers-Binder-Program/300546833450466

Review of Binders

https://chestbinders.wordpress.com/

STP (Stand-to-pee)

Free To M Prosthetics

http://www.freetomprosthetics.com

Transthetics

http://transthetics.com/

FTM Essentials

http://www.ftmessentials.com/collections/stp-devices

APPENDIX V
CONFERENCES AND PROGRAMS

Camp Aranu'tiq

http://www.camparanutiq.org/

Creating Change

http://www.creatingchange.org/

Esprit

http://www.espritconf.com/

Fantasia Fair

http://www.fantasiafair.org/

First Event

http://firstevent.org/

Gender Odyssey

http://www.genderodyssey.org/

Gender Spectrum

https://www.genderspectrum.org/

Keystone Conference

http://www.keystone-conference.org/

Out and Equal

http://www.outandequal.org/

Philadelphia Transgender Health Conference

http://www.trans-health.org/

Midwest Bisexual Lesbian Gay Transgender Ally College Conference

https://saapps.illinoisstate.edu/dos/mblgtacc2015/

Transcending Boundaries

http://transcendingboundaries.org/

TransOhio Symposium

http://www.transohio.org/wordpress/

APPENDIX VI
SURGERY AND FORUMS

SURGERY

MTF Surgery

http://www.mtfsurgery.net/

FTM Surgery

http://www.ftmsurgery.net/

Transbucket

http://www.transbucket.com/

Phalloplasty

http://www.phallo.net/

Metoidioplasty

http://www.metoidioplasty.net/

ONLINE FORUMS

Yahoo has many forums. Search the site for various groups. Some examples are below. These groups have personal accounts and photos from people who have gone through various kinds of surgery. It is a great support/networking system. You will need a Yahoo account to join these groups.

FTM-Trans

FTM Early Transitioning

FTM Metoidioplasty

FTM Surgery Support

FTM Phalloplasty Info

FTM Surgery Info

FTM Centurion Surgery

The Deciding Line

APPENDIX VII
BOOKS

SELF-HELP AND SUCCESS

The 7 Habits of Highly Effective Teens, Sean Covey

The 6 Most Important Decisions You'll Ever Make, Sean Covey

Failing Forward, John Maxwell

NONFICTION

Becoming a Visible Man by Jamison Green

Beyond Magenta: Transgender Teens Speak Out, Susan Kuklin

Body Alchemy: Transsexual Portraits, Loren Cameron

Facial Feminization Surgery, Douglas K, Ousterhout, M.D.

Feminizing Men–A Guide for Males to Achieve Maximum Feminization, Barbara Deloto and Thomas Newgen

Finding Masculinity: Female to Male Transition in Adulthood, A. Walker and E. J. P. Lundberg

Hung Jury: Testimonies of Genital Surgery by Transsexual Men, Trystan Cotten (Editor)

Just Add Hormones: An Insider's Guide to the Transsexual Experience, Matt Kailey

Letters for My Brothers: Transitional Wisdom in Retrospect, Meghan M. Rohrer and Zander Keig (Editors)

Letters for My Sisters: Transitional Wisdom in Retrospect, Andrea James and Deanne Thornton (Editors)

Manning Up: Transsexual Men on Finding Brotherhood, Family and Themselves, Zander Keig and Mitch Kellaway (Editors)

My New Gender Workbook: A Step-by-Step Guide to Achieving World Peace through Gender Anarchy and Sex Positivity, Kate Bornstein

Now What? A Handbook for Families with Transgender Children, Rex Butt

Redefining Realness: My Path to Womanhood, Identity, Love, & So Much More, Janet Mock

Rethinking Normal: A Memoir in Transition, Katie Rain Hill

Second Son: Transitioning Toward My Destiny, Life, and Love, Ryan Sallans

She's Not There: A Life in Two Genders, Jennifer Finney Boylan

Some Assembly Required: The Not-So-Secret Life of a Transgender Teen, Arin Andrews

The Nearest Exit May Be Behind You, S. Bear Bergman

Trans Bodies, Trans Selves edited by Laura Erickson-Schroth

Transgender Lives, Kirstin Cronn-Mills

Transgender Warriors, Leslie Feinberg

YOUNG ADULT FICTION

A Boy Like Me, Jennie Wood

Beauty Queens, Libba Bray

Being Emily, Rachel Gold

Beautiful Music for Ugly Children, Kirstin Cronn-Mills

First Spring Grass Fire, Rae Spoon

I Am J, Cris Beam

If You Could Be Mine, Sara Farizan

If We Shadows, D.E. Atwood

I Know Very Well How I Got My Name, Elliot Deline

Just Girls, Rachel Gold

Luna, Julie Anne Peters

Parrotfish, Ellen Wittlinger

Roving Pack, Sassafras Lowrey

Run, Clarissa, Run, Rachel Eliason

Supervillainz, Alicia E. Goranson

The Trans-Fer Student, Elise Himes

Wandering Son, Shimura Takako

APPENDIX VIII
REPORTS AND SURVEYS

Injustice at every turn: A Report of the National Transgender Discrimination Survey

http://www.thetaskforce.org/static_html/downloads/reports/reports/ntds_full.pdf

Injustice at every turn: State reports of the National Transgender Discrimination

http://www.thetaskforce.org/injustice-every-turn-state-reports-national-transgender-discrimination-survey/

Transgender Equality and the Federal Government

http://transequality.org/federal_gov.html

APPENDIX IX

HORMONE CHANGE MEASUREMENT CHART

BEGINNING DATE				
MEASUREMENT DATES				
LIST HORMONES AMOUNTS==>				
Height				
Weight				
MEASUREMENTS				
Waist				
HIps				
Arms				
Biceps Flexed				
Biceps Not flexed				
Left				
RIght				
Bust/Bra Sixe				
Chest				
Thighs				
Left				
Right				
Calves				
Left				
Right				
Ring Size				
Shoe Size				
Pants Size				
Dress Size				
Undershirt				
Underwear				
Ankles				
Wrist				
Finger To Wrist				
Neck				
Head				
Chin Strap (Ear to Ear under chin)				
Foot Length				
Foot Width				
Receed Forehead to Nose Bridge				
Right				
Left				
Palm				
Right				
Left				
SOME MEASUREMENTS ARE FOR WOMEN - SOME ARE FOR MEN				

APPENDIX X
HORMONE EFFECTS/EXPECTED TIME

The Standards of Care VERSION 7

World Professional Association for Transgender Health

EFFECTS AND EXPECTED TIME COURSE OF FEMINIZING HORMONES A

Effect	Expected onset B	Expected maximum effect B
Body fat redistribution	3–6 months	2–5 years
Decreased muscle mass/strength	3–6 months	1–2 years C
Softening of skin/decreased oiliness	3–6 months	Unknown
Decreased libido	1–3 months	1–2 years
Decreased spontaneous erections	1–3 months	3–6 months
Male sexual dysfunction	Variable	Variable
Breast growth	3–6 months	2–3 years
Decreased testicular volume	3–6 months	2–3 years
Decreased sperm production	Variable	Variable
Thinning and slowed growth of body and facial hair	6–12 months	> 3 years D
Male pattern baldness	No regrowth, loss stops 1–3 months	1–2 years

A Adapted with permission from Hembree et al. (2009). Copyright 2009, The Endocrine Society.
B Estimates represent published and unpublished clinical observations.
C Significantly dependent on amount of exercise.
D Complete removal of male facial and body hair requires electrolysis, laser treatment, or both.

The Standards of Care VERSION 7

World Professional Association for Transgender Health

EFFECTS AND EXPECTED TIME COURSE OF MASCULINIZING HORMONES [A]

Effect	**Expected onset** [B]	**Expected maximum effect** [B]
Skin oiliness/acne	1–6 months	1–2 years
Facial/body hair growth	3–6 months	3–5 years
Scalp hair loss	>12 months [C]	Variable
Increased muscle mass/strength	6–12 months	2–5 years [D]
Body fat redistribution	3–6 months	2–5 years
Cessation of menses	2–6 months	n/a
Clitoral enlargement	3–6 months	1–2 years
Vaginal atrophy	3–6 months	1–2 years
Deepened voice	3–12 months	1–2 years

A Adapted with permission from Hembree et al.(2009). Copyright 2009, The Endocrine Society.
B Estimates represent published and unpublished clinical observations.
C Highly dependent on age and inheritance; may be minimal.
D Significantly dependent on amount of exercise.

The Standards of Care VERSION 7

World Professional Association for Transgender Health

RISKS ASSOCIATED WITH HORMONE THERAPY. BOLDED ITEMS ARE CLINICALLY SIGNIFICANT

Risk Level	**Feminizing hormones**	**Masculinizing hormones**
Likely increased risk	Venous thromboembolic disease A Gallstones Elevated liver enzymes Weight gain Hypertriglyceridemia	Polycythemia Weight gain Acne Androgenic alopecia (balding) Sleep apnea
Likely increased risk with presence of Additional risk factors B	Cardiovasc	
Possible increased risk	Hypertension Hyperprolactinemia or prolactinoma	Elevated liver enzymes Hyperlipidemia
Possible increased risk with presence of additional risk factors B	Type 2 diabetes B	Destabilization of certain psychiatric disorders C Cardiovascular disease Hypertension Type 2 diabetes
No increased risk or inconclusive	Breast cancer	Loss of bone density Breast cancer Cervical cancer Ovarian cancer Uterine cancer

* Note: Risk is greater with oral estrogen administration than with transdermal estrogen administration.

A Risk is greater with oral estrogen administration than with transdermal estrogen administration.

B Additional risk factors include age.

C Includes bipolar, schizoaffective, and other disorders that may include manic or psychotic symptoms. This adverse event appears to be associated with higher doses or supraphysiologic blood levels of testosterone.

APPENDIX XI
PARENTS' GUIDE

OMG! My Child (May Be) Transgender!

Take a Deep Breath

Right now you may be feeling confused, angry, and skeptical. You may be in disbelief that your child could be transgender. But you should know this: if your child has come to you and disclosed their thoughts about feeling different inside from their outside appearance, you should feel *great*. After all, this means that as a parent, you've done your job.

First and foremost, your child came to you and was able to talk to you. *Please keep that in mind*!

As difficult as it may seem to keep your feelings in check, it is very important to hear what your child is saying right now. They are concerned only with their own feelings and may not recognize your fears and concerns. They cannot understand how difficult it is for you to view your daughter as your son, or vice versa. It is very important for you to try not to respond negatively because your child may never talk about this with you again.

Is My Child *Really* Transgender?

While nothing is cast in stone, there are two strong indicators that your child is, indeed, transgender. The first one is the discomfort they feel with certain aspects of their bodies, often their genitals. The second is their desire to be perceived by others as the gender they feel they are.

By the time a child has finally told their parents they are transgender, they likely feel impatient and want to physically transition as soon as possible. They believe that they have been suffering for years, and are not likely taking into account that their parents are having a hard time accepting their need to be the other sex.

Why Are They Telling Me Now?

Younger children, being as creative and imaginative as they are, feel that their gender will somehow work itself out. But as your child gets older, the discordance with who they are inside, and who they appear to be on the outside, often becomes more disturbing. Puberty is often a sore reminder that the feelings won't resolve themselves. An array of emotions can accompany this process including depression, hopelessness, anger, disappointment, and fear, among others.

A child—as for anyone—will find it hard to explain their feelings. They may be worrying that they will lose friends and be cast out by their parents. They may dislike seeing themselves in the mirror because they are disappointed that their outer appearance does not match their inner self. They may feel out of place in the bathroom and try to avoid outdoor activities like going to the beach. They may even try temporarily to please others, but the desire to be their true self will return.

Initial Fears

At this point, you are likely feeling cautious and are concerned about the safety of your child. As a parent, there are many things that can go through your mind. One may be a fear of the harassment your child could face, or even that the harassment they already face could worsen. But remember: If a child has support from home, this can help increase their confidence and put them at ease. This, in turn, may help others at school to be more accepting.

You may fear the physical harm others can enact. But consider the reality that youth who are not allowed to transition run a risk of depression, self-hatred, and perhaps even substance abuse; these are all indicators of potential self-harm.

You may fear that your child is mentally ill. It is possible that, in rare cases, that child has a simultaneously occurring mental illness *in addition to identifying as transgender*. But remember: being transgender is not, in and of itself, a mental disorder. And if a child believes that they are transgender, they *are*. A gender identity therapist can help your child clarify whether this is true or not.

But My Child Is Too Young!

Gender identity is an inherent knowledge one feels inside. It isn't like wanting a bicycle one day and then changing one's mind. For most children, being transgender is a constant, disruptive reminder that their body and mind are not in sync. Let this knowledge put your mind at ease about your child possibly going back-and-forth on their convictions because they are too young, or because they are being rebellious or seeking attention.

Finally, you may fear that your child will someday regret transitioning. However, my experience has shown that teens who feel strongly that they are transgender are most likely going to continue feeling this way into adulthood. The vast majority of post-transition people never regret the decision they have made. (*Side note*: You can expect that if your child is under the age of 16, reversible hormonal interventions will be considered. After that age, cross-gender hormones will be the most likely option).

By allowing your child to transition at an early age, they will be able to begin living their life as they feel they should. They can be more focused on their life goals instead of constantly thinking about their body. With your help, they can build a solid foundation of confidence and self-worth.

Is My Child Actually Gay?

You might prefer believing that your child is a non-transgender gay man or lesbian woman because in today's society sexual minorities are accepted more easily than gender minorities. But just as one does not choose to be gay or lesbian, one doesn't choose to be transgender. Further, sexual attraction and gender identity are different aspects of the self; transgender people may go on to identify as straight, gay, lesbian, or bisexual *in addition* to being transgender.

In the beginning, some children may identify as lesbian or gay before they come to realize that they are transgender. This is partly because our society tells us that gender nonconformity (e.g. dressing masculinely or femininely, or being attracted to the "opposite" gender) is always a part of sexual orientation. If your child "comes out" to you twice—first as gay or lesbian, then as transgender—know that the confusion doesn't lie with them, but with the labels they've inherited from society.

How Will the Rest of the Family React?

Much of the discomfort you may be feeling emerges from society's ideas concerning transgender/transsexual people *[see Terms and Definitions in this section for more explanation of these terms]*. You may have been taught that these identities are forms of sickness, or they are perverted or immoral. However, as the parent of a transgender child, you need to free yourself from negative beliefs and start to educate yourself. At the end of the day, your child being who they truly are is what matters most. And when they begin to feel happier, you will begin to be happy for them as well.

Certainly, it would be great for every parent to be immediately accepting and willing to educate themselves on how to move forward with the best interests and happiness of their child in mind. However, this is not the case in many families.

There is often one willing parent and one parent who is obstinate and just cannot face the facts. Keep the lines of communication open with the rest of your family, including siblings and a spouse (if applicable), but continue to do what you think is best for your child.

Initial Reactions Will Not Last Forever

While it's possible that your child informing you of their transgender identity can put a strain on the family—other siblings may or may not be open to change; maybe a father or mother says they want nothing to do with their transgender child—recognize that this may not stay the same forever. This is not a situation to start blaming either spouse for their initial reactions, because no spouse is responsible for unexpected situations.

There are many families in which transgender children end up homeless. Your awareness of such possibilities can help prevent that from happening to your child. Let them impel you to find support outside the family *[See Finding Support below]*.

How Will Others React?

OMG, what will others think? It is natural to be concerned about the reactions of others in your family and extended circles. But in the best interests of your child, you will need to get your feelings in check and educate yourself before you discuss their identity with people outside of your household.

When you do eventually speak to others, it is important to initially acknowledge their discomfort and tell them you felt the same way in the beginning—but that you've decided to keep an open mind out of love for your child. You can ask them for their support and also state that you will entertain any questions that they have about your child's transition. During this time, you will begin to see that not only is your child transitioning, but you are as well.

Feelings of Loss

Address the fact that you may go through a grieving process yourself. In some ways, this is a loss (or a symbolic "death") to you. These feelings emerge, in part, from realizing that certain hopes and dreams for your child's future will not be fulfilled. You wanted a little girl who would grow to become a woman, and now you've found that you're going to have a son (or vice versa). It is important that you take as much time as you need to be able to accept this loss, and take any self-care measures you normally do when grieving.

Let your child know that you are experiencing feelings of a loss. This can help them begin to understand what a difficult adjustment their transition may be for you. But beyond informing them, *it is not your child's responsibility to help you deal with this loss.* There are support groups for parents facing the same issues that will be able to help you deal with hard emotions and other concerns.

Finding Support

The advice you are currently reading is not meant to fulfill all your support needs. Reading online is only a beginning. The good news is that in today's world, there are many viable options for education and help. There is a growing need for accurate and compassionate information for families with transgender children, and the world is responding, albeit slowly.

The Internet offers a plethora of information that can be put to good use. However, use common sense rather than placing belief in everything you read. There are many gender therapists, transgender health conferences, PFLAG meetings,[25] and doctors that offer valid information. (Also refer to the APPENDICES in this book.)

Above all, the most helpful step you can take is to keep an unbiased attitude toward whatever your child may be telling you. Do not be afraid to ask non-judgmental questions. While it may be hard to hold back everything you want to say, you must remember that if your first response to your child is an objection, then you can expect stubborn behavior when engaging in any future discussions. They may not be willing to discuss this matter again, and will likely feel rejected, or possibly even unloved, by you.

Moving Forward

It is essential to realize that there is not an exact answer for every issue that may come up. So it is crucial for you to get the appropriate help from a qualified therapist who will be able to guide you concerning your emotions and shed light on the journeys transgender children undertake. In so doing, you will become supportive of your own child and enable them to build self-confidence and become stronger as they forge ahead.

This short guide has been prepared to simply provide an introduction. You will encounter much more information as you move forward, particularly assistance related to your individual child and their unique needs.

Most importantly, remember this: ***Don't panic.***

You still have a child who is capable of living a happy and productive life, provided you are there as a parent to help support and assist them. It is by no means an

25 www.pflag.org

easy journey, but one that can definitely be successful and positive if approached with forethought and compassion.

TERMS & DEFINITIONS

The following definitions are fairly simple but do sometimes sound confusing. Imagine now the confusion a child must feel when they appear one way but feel another and those around them are using words and pronouns that do not match their true gender.

Transgender

A transgender person's internal gender identity does not match their body's biological sex (or what some may refer to as *"assigned at birth"* sex). "Transgender" may be used as an individual identity for someone who wishes to transition their gender socially and/or physically, but is sometimes also used as an umbrella term that encompasses those who desire physical transition and other gender nonconforming (GNC) people, such as genderfluid and genderqueer people or cross-dressers *(see definitions that follow and the full glossary in Appendix I).*

Transsexual

A more antiquated term, "transsexual" refers to a more specific transgender identity; when a transsexual person's internal gender identity does not match their body's biological sex, they wish to undertake *physical* measures, with the aid of hormones and/or gender confirming surgeries (sometimes referred to as *"Sexual Reassignment Surgeries"* SRS), to correct their alignment between body and mind. This term separates transsexual people from other transgender people who do not need medical intervention to feel whole.

FTM and MTF

Female-to-male (FTM) transgender people are born with female biology but know themselves to be male, and wish to be perceived as such socially (including the use of male pronouns like *"he"* and *"his"*). Male-to-female (MTF) transgender people are born with male biology but know themselves to be female, and wish to be perceived as such socially (including the use of female pronouns like *"she"* and *"hers"*).He wants to have female anatomy and be called by female pronouns.

Gender Identity

Gender identity is an inner sense of being female, male, neither, or both. By the age of 3, children often have a clear sense of either being male or female. Most the time their identity conforms to their biological sex; whether this is the case or the child is transgender, society instills in them rules about one should conform to their birth sex.

Gender Expression

Gender expression is the presentation of self to others as masculine, feminine, both, or neither. Some of expression's aspects include mannerisms or movement, dressing and grooming, and possibly certain behaviors or interests. Unfortunately, children whose gender expressions do not meet with what society feels they should be are usually mistreated. Children learn quickly how to try to fit in. However, gender nonconforming (GNC) children will likely continue to act and behave in accordance with their interests despite these attempts, and despite the consequences of running counter to what is expected of them.

Sexual Orientation

Sexual orientation is about romantic and sexual attraction; it is not a choice. Attraction lies on a broad spectrum. A person can be attracted to just women, or just men, or both—and these can shift over a lifetime. Sexual orientation has nothing to do with gender identity or gender expression; orientation is about how one finds *others* attractive, while gender identity and expression are about how one perceives and manifests the *self*. Everyone has *both a sexual orientation and a gender identity.*

Genderfluid or Genderqueer

Genderfluid or genderqueer people internally understand their gender identity as falling outside the binary construct of "male" and "female." They may feel, and perhaps struggle to convey to others, that their gender is a mix of both, varies from day to day, is neither or beyond, or something else entirely. They may request that others refer to them with gender-neutral pronouns such as *"they."*

Pansexual

Pansexual people may be sexually attracted to individuals who identify as male or female; however, they may also be attracted to those who identify as intersex, third-gender, androgynous, transsexual, or the many other sexual and gender identities.

Cross-dressing

Cross-dressing people wear clothing traditionally worn by another gender. They may vary with how completely or often they cross-dress, but are usually comfortable with their assigned biological sex and do not wish to physically change it.

You have a wonderful life
ahead of you. Stay Strong
and follow your dreams!
Seth

Seth Rainess is a writer, motivational speaker, and life coach.

Seth speaks from a profound place of knowing who he is. Born in the 1950s, a time when social consciousness had not yet evolved into today's levels of acceptance, Seth has experienced what many trans teens are feeling and he offers his perspectives as a man from a previous generation. He's witnessed firsthand how minds have become less judgmental and more open over time. This, among other changes, allowed him, over time, to move forward with his gender transition.

He wrote *Real Talk for Teens: Jump-Start Guide to Gender Transitioning and Beyond* in order to present trans teens with a foundation for transitioning, and a unique perspective on what it takes to be successful in today's world. He draws on his rich life history, to offer youth and parents an emotional road-map and physical timeline through gender transition and the exciting life that can lie beyond.

Seth hopes that *Real Talk for Teens* will help trans youth to transition successfully and go on to live a productive and happy life.

Seth holds a master of science in both psychology and rehab counseling from Boston University. He speaks in seminars and school assemblies for trans youth and conducts diversity training for faculty in high schools and universities. He also provides workshops for health professionals. He is comfortable in large settings or small intimate groups and draws on his extensive knowledge from years of research, community advocacy, and personal experience.

A committed proponent for gender neutral equality, he also devotes some of his time as a Jersey Shore PFLAG facilitator, a member of World Professional Association of Transgender Health (WPATH), volunteer for Gay Lesbian Straight Education Network (GLSEN). Combining his thirty years of experience working in the business sector and nonprofit organizations, with his passion for helping trans youth, he is able to offer wisdom from his own life in discussing the surprises, worries, joys and rewards of transitioning for youth today.

His website offers additional information and resources and provides an atmosphere in which both prospective transgender youth and their parents can feel safe enough to ask their most personal questions without shame. To hire Seth, go to www.sethrainess.com.

YOUR LIFE IS WAITING FOR YOU. EMBRACE AND LIVE IT TO THE FULLEST!

ANOTHER BOOK FROM SETH - GREAT GIFT FOR CAT LOVERS
ON AMAZON.COM

Want to be a Real Man? Express Yourself! | Seth Rainess | TEDxWilmington
https://www.youtube.com/watch?v=bRXz4d3k_xo

Made in the USA
Middletown, DE
28 April 2021